ARMAMENTS AND ARBITRATION

ARMAMENTS
AND
ARBITRATION

OR

THE PLACE OF FORCE
IN THE INTERNATIONAL RELATIONS OF STATES

BY

A. T. MAHAN, D.C.L., LL.D.
CAPTAIN, U. S. N. (RETIRED)

AUTHOR OF "THE INFLUENCE OF SEA-POWER UPON HISTORY"
"THE INTEREST OF AMERICA IN SEA-POWER" "THE
INTEREST OF AMERICA IN INTERNATIONAL
CONDITIONS" "THE LIFE OF FARRAGUT"
"THE LIFE OF NELSON" "FROM
SAIL TO STEAM" ETC.

KENNIKAT PRESS
Port Washington, N. Y./London

CONTENTS

PREFACE

THE ten articles contained in this work were contributed, with one exception, to the *North American Review*, during the years 1911 and 1912. The exception is the seventh—The Panama Canal and Sea Power in the Pacific—which appeared in the *Century Magazine* for June, 1911.

The first six were planned as a series, intended to present the arguments, too frequently ignored, that neither Arbitration in a general sense, nor Arbitration in the more specific form of judicial decision based upon a code of law, can always take the place, either practically or beneficially, of the processes and results obtained by the free play of natural forces. Of these forces national efficiency is a chief element; and armament, being the representative of the national strength, is the exponent. This leading thought finds expression in the second title (subtitle) of the book—The Place of Force in the International Relations of States.

The author takes occasion to make his acknowledgments and thanks to the proprietors and editors of the *North American Review*, and of the *Century Magazine*, for the permission to republish which they have kindly given.

A. T. MAHAN.

September, 1912.

ARMAMENTS AND ARBITRATION

ARMAMENTS AND ARBITRATION

INTRODUCTION

As is the case with all political doctrines, the theory of Arbitration possesses a principle of development.   It is necessary to take this into account in order properly to estimate the direction in which arbitration is tending, and the possible goal at which it may arrive, unless diverted by modifying influences not immediately apparent.   Like the observations of a comet's positions which enable a probable calculation of its orbit, we already have in the past and present of arbitration certain fairly ascertained points whence to infer its general future tendency if left to itself.

First may be noted that one distinct influence so far observable is toward undermining the principle of independent nationality, which has played so great and beneficent a part in the history of European civilization for the past four hundred years.   This may be a good thing, or it may not.   It may connote a real advance, or it may be a symptom of reaction.

I

In either case it involves a profound modification of what may be called, not inaccurately, the constitutional basis of the sovereignty of the State, upon which rest the international relations of the community of countries comprised in European civilization. It may be desirable that this principle undergo essential modification. It is possible that we have before us a period of transition, wherein the strong sentiment of nationality may prove simply the conservative force which by delaying shall steady the onward movement toward the logical consummation of arbitration without finally preventing it; but in any case it is essential to note the tendency clearly and to keep it in mind continuously.

In its origins Arbitration was an instrument in the workshop of diplomacy of which national governments availed themselves freely at will. Whatever the method adopted, the distinguishing feature in that past was the perfect liberty to use or not to use in the particular instance. It may be said that the same is the case now; but evidently it is not. Not to speak of the coercive influence of public emotion, perhaps more in love with the name than comprehensive of the facts, yet extremely powerful, the tendency distinctly is to increase limitations upon the freedom of governments to use or to reject arbitration. Treaties even of unlimited obligation to arbitrate have been made; while the omission of phrases defining previous classified reservations, such as "vital interests and national honor," is clearly a long stride in the same direction. The recently framed treaties between the United States and France, and the United States and Great Britain, took a further step, imposing the arbitration of all questions susceptible of judicial decision by the principles of law and equity. This was equivalent to eliminating certain reservations previously maintained; retaining freedom of action only in disputes to which no existing law could be applied. The course of the Senate in emasculating the treaties, whether right or wrong in the particular instance, was an example of national sentiment retarding the progress of arbitration, by rejecting a proposed method. In the debate, the principle of recourse to arbitration as an instrument to be used voluntarily was expressly indorsed; but certain restrictions upon the national freedom of choice, to use it or not as each case arose, were rejected.

The whole incident, from the speech of President Taft, in December, 1910, through that of Sir Edward Grey, the British Foreign Secretary, March 13, 1911, up to the signature of the treaties and their subsequent modification by the Senate of the United States, illustrates the facts indicated—the facts of progress, of its general direction, and of the modifying element noted above. National sentiment, the sentiment of national independence, freedom to act in the future as future interests might require, dictated the course of the Senate. This is entirely obvious,—beyond dispute, although disputed,—for the principle of judicial arbitration was implicitly accepted. The change in the text of the treaties determined only that the decision as to "justiciable" or "non-justiciable" should rest with the government of the future day; not be determined for it by the possibly imperfect valuations of to-day.

There is, then, a clear tendency in arbitration to progress from a means to be used voluntarily to one that shall be more compulsive. Are there again conditions discernible which tend to render compulsion more frequent and more urgent, thus narrowing further the scope of national liberty of action as to recourse to arbitration? If so, do these indications point to a further unchecked movement in the same direction? or do they rather indicate that already nations feel that movement has been either too far or too fast, and that in the interest not merely of the particular state, but of the world generally, it is time to call a halt; to rest where we are; to refuse to permit the present to pledge further the unknown future? The action of Italy in Tripoli; that taken by France, England, Spain, and ultimately Germany, in Morocco; the case of the United States with reference to Colombia, Panama, and the Panama Canal Zone; all these may be cited as instances in which previous arbitration stipulations might have—it is claimed in some quarters actually have—seriously fettered, if not prevented, the national measures, because the national independence

4

of action, which is the corner-stone of international law, had been mortgaged in whole or in part.

On its present line of development, the theory of arbitration points to a system for the community of nations resembling that which Socialism would impose within the single state; and, in fact, Socialism as a theory progresses logically from the regulation of the national social order to advocate the abolition of national distinctions. To be consistent—perhaps not the highest of qualities—arbitration should undertake not merely to settle disputes which directly threaten war, but also to rectify the concrete inequalities, deriving from existing law or prescription, which place nations on different planes of advantage, and thus constitute the jealousies and antagonisms in which wars find their origin; just as social inequalities are provoking a demand for state regulation as against individual possession or achievement. The corner-stone of labor organization is the creation of an artificial equality among members, coupled with a determination to spread equality still farther by coercing individuals into unions. Thus compulsory arbitration between members of the nation, between private citizens, is to be instituted by the government, modifying the differences of estate which arise from conditions either natural or artificial, and thus cause the conflict of interest between different sections of the community.

Is the arbitration tribunal which the nations have set up to become thus a central power re-

scriptive rights. If mutual consent be of the essence of arbitration, it is an avowal that force remains the determining factor. For the state that possesses markedly superior organized force may consent to arbitrate, but it will remain the judge in its own case as to whether it will do so or not.

In brief, the question between armaments and arbitration in the present stage of the development of the world is that between reaching an ultimate equilibrium by the play of natural forces, of which armaments are the ultimate expression, or by an artificial method based upon law and equity, or custom, which often will have ceased to be applicable. It will be admitted, of course, that all human interference with a natural course of events introduces an artificial factor, and that human progress is a resultant of natural forces and artificial interventions. If the immigration from eastern Asia into America, a natural movement, were not qualified by the artificial obstacle of American resistance, few thoughtful persons can doubt that the North American continent west of the Rocky Mountains would be Asiatic in population a century hence.

In this our day the development of the world may be said to present two principal factors: European civilization, and the civilizations, or barbarisms, as the case may be, which are not European in origin or derivation. As regards energy, especially organized energy, the European is far the most powerful; and the demonstration of that energy lies not

8

only in the vast social and industrial progresses accomplished, but in armament, the ultimate exponent of national independence and power. The existing competitions between European nations sustain not only armaments, but the spirit of which armaments are the expression. These are the necessary reliance of a highly organized, less numerous civilization, meeting external conditions where numbers are much greater; and where the power of mere endurance also is superior, because the social system is far less complicated, and the individual is accustomed to hardnesses and privations which with us have in great measure disappeared. To borrow a simile from the natural sciences, momentum, the ultimate force of impact in a collision, is composed of mass and of velocity. In the matter before us, mass is on the side of the non-European. The equivalent of velocity, energy, is on the side of Europe; the term Europe including in this respect its offshoot, America.

In the future processes of adjustment, in which we doubtless shall see the superior organization of European civilization imitated as it has been successfully in Japan, it is of the first importance that the European family of states retain in full the power of national self-assertion, of which the sentiment of nationality is the spirit and armaments the embodiment; for so only, by the national force of the several states in active competition with one another, can the force of the whole be depended upon for maintaining itself, and thus ultimately reducing by assimilation the opposing external forces. Eliminate, if you can, the competition between the several nationalities, so as to suppress the armaments; substitute for these the artificial system of compulsory arbitration, and disarmament; and you will have realized a socialistic community of states, in which the powers of individual initiative, of nations and of men, the great achievement of our civilization so far, will gradually be atrophied. The result may be that European civilization will not survive, having lost the fighting energy which heretofore has been inherent in its composition.

It is evident that Arbitration and Force represent diametrically opposed ideas. It does not follow, however, that they are mutually destructive, any more than are centripetal and centrifugal. The opposition may result in the ultimate disappearance of armed forces, as an element of international relations; but force, the organized force of the community as the means of assuring its will, is and must remain the basis of social order so long as evil exists to be repressed. Meantime, no one conversant with the present state of the world at large can doubt that extensive political readjustments are inevitable. Many are already in progress. We need only to name Morocco, Tripoli, Turkey, Persia, China, coupling with these names the political unrest of the Eastern World and the aggressive advance of the Western, not in arms only,

but in industrial enterprises all over the globe, to
realize how great the problems are. As one indication of the tendency of the movements connoted,
let it be cited incidentally that when France occupied
Algiers, in 1830, the total trade of the country, export and import, was less than a million dollars.
In 1910 it was two hundred millions. Similarly,
since the French protectorate over Tunis was established, in 1881, the commerce of that dependency
has risen from eight million dollars to forty. It
ought to be needless to point out the immense social and economical improvements which necessarily underlie such commercial development. For instance, in Tunis the French since 1882 have built
two thousand miles of good roads. The trade of
Morocco to-day is about thirty millions.

The following papers, contributed—with one
exception—to *The North American Review* during
the years 1911 and 1912, form a summary examination of certain of the several factors involved in the
contrasted methods of Armament and Arbitration,
with all that the two words imply— force on the one
hand, law on the other. In the writer's appreciation,
armament represents the aggregation of the natural
forces inherent in any community. This is especially true to-day, because in the strong rivalry
and oppositions internal to the system of European
civilization the armaments are a gage of the capaci-
ties of the people not only to do, in all the phases of
national activity, but to bear—a no less important

element of national power. Arbitration, on the other hand, connotes law as its ultimate expression; for, although it often deals merely with facts, as a jury does, its decision has the force of law, while in many cases the decision itself must depend upon points of law. There is an element of truth in the phrase, "Law instead of War"; for this is the antithesis between arbitration and armament. The trouble with law is that, being artificial and often of long date, it frequently is inapplicable to a present dispute; that is, its decision is incompatible with existing conditions, although it may rest on grounds legally unimpeachable. The settlement, therefore, is insecure, its foundations are not solid; whereas in the long run the play of natural forces reaches an adjustment corresponding to the fundamental facts of the case.

One has only to note the horror with which a lawyer naturally regards such action as that of Italy in Tripoli, or of the United States at Panama, to recognize that a permanent conclusion—which spells peace—cannot be reached by legal definitions when they contravene essential facts. Apparently, the question at stake in such instances, seen from the legal point of view, is one merely of property rights. If war already exists, law is quite willing that the property should be taken; but short of war the transaction stands condemned by law. Nevertheless, the legal tenure of a nation, its prescriptive right to some district, unless it be accompanied by effective occupation and utilization, must go under, if it contravenes the necessities of the world, or of another state; but international law is not competent so to decide, nor is an arbitral court. If it be proposed to confer that power upon an international tribunal, a kind of power of eminent domain, will it be limited to the considerations of utilization? Or must it be empowered to consider also other asserted rights, political in character, as the demand of certain classes in Egypt that the country be free of British control, or in the Philippines of American?

There can be little doubt that these matters will be settled in a manner far more advantageous to the world by leaving them to the play of natural forces. It will be better to depend upon the great armaments, as institutions maintaining peace, which they have done effectually for forty years in Europe itself, and not to demoralize the European peoples by the flood of socialistic measures which will follow upon the release to a beneficiary system of the sums now spent on armament. It is not worth while to cajole ourselves with the belief that money economized from armament will be money saved to the State. The city of New York maintains no armaments, yet it will hardly be cited as a pattern of economical administration. The consolidated Roman Empire with its Pax Romana is not a wholly happy augury for a future of peace dependent upon a central court and general disarmament. All that European civilization has to depend upon for its supremacy is its energy, of which international competition and armament are not only expressions, but essential elements —factors. When these fail and fall the end will be at hand.

I

ARMAMENTS AND ARBITRATION

To those who are accustomed to note European news with somewhat more particularity than is given by the cable despatches of the American press, it must have appeared a singular coincidence that along with the telegraphic message conveying the now famous speech (March 13, 1911) of Sir Edward Grey, the British Secretary of Foreign Affairs, advocating unlimited arbitration between Great Britain and the United States, there arrived by mail the detailed information that the German Parliament had passed the bill for an annual increase of their already formidable army, for each succeeding year, up to and including 1916.

The vote for this significant measure stood 247 to 63, or, put in terms more readily comprehended at a glance, as four to one; and the small minority was composed, with only three exceptions, of Socialists and Poles,[1] the latter of whom stand in

---

[1] To be perfectly exact, it should be mentioned that there were eleven abstentions; a fact which makes a very different impression according as it is stated that there were eleven or that there were *only* eleven.

relation to the German government much as the Nationalist party of Ireland stands toward Great Britain—permanently disaffected as long as present conditions last.

It may be fairly said, therefore, after making all allowance for the peculiar state of the franchise in the chief state of the Empire—Prussia—that this increase of the army is a popular measure; that it is not merely the act of a government, esteemed by many to be arbitrary and self-willed, but the voice of a mighty people, satisfied for the time being that the national interests require augmentation of an army already proverbial for numbers and efficiency —an army which may fairly be said to hold the casting vote, when opposing European forces approach equality even remotely.

It is unnecessary here to enumerate the occasions on which this force has been exerted, or where it has been checked by other combinations, within the ten years past; but it is well to note the general fact that organized military force, even when used, does not necessarily mean war in its horrors. It is war without bloodshed; a result which is the great and only real justification of military preparation. Witness the American War of Secession, with its immense losses. In this both sides stood at the beginning without any preparation, as compared with the immense development and organization, military and naval, which the course of the contest brought into being. The German Empire, which owes its existence to its army, has, thanks also to its army, known forty years of unbroken peace, of the sheathed sword.

Not the least striking feature of this new accumulation of armament in the midst of peace is that it is for a term of coming years during which there is no certainty, even under a continuance of peace conditions, that the revenue will meet the consequent increased expenditure. To quote a phrase attributed recently to an American statesman, this may be bad economics; yet it is evidently considered good politics. But it is not for the army only that debt, or the possibility of debt, is contemplated. The huge advance in numbers and in size of ships of the German navy is being met by the same resource. Broadly stated, without taking account of the details of ordinary and extraordinary expenditure, the bill for new naval construction, as distinguished from running expenses, is met by loans— by an annual increase of debt. By this means Germany has progressed to the second place among the naval powers of the world, being exceeded only by Great Britain, which so far pays for its naval shipbuilding out of current revenue. It seems scarcely necessary to say that, after all allowance for wealth still much exceeding that of Germany, Great Britain owes this ability to her watery bulwarks, which enable her to depend upon a much less numerous army. It is also, perhaps, worth noting that the immense debt of Great Britain was contracted in establishing, by military means, the territorial, commercial, and industrial conditions which underlay her long-continued financial supremacy; that the debt was in the nature of an investment, not barren of returns.

In the British House of Commons, the First Lord of the Admiralty, the civil head of the British navy —corresponding to our Secretary of the Navy—has stated (March 16, 1911), in answer to a question, that, according to the programmes so far adopted, Great Britain on April 1st, 1914, would have completed 22 Dreadnoughts and 9 Invincibles; Germany, 16 Dreadnoughts, 5 Invincibles; the United States, 12 Dreadnoughts, no Invincibles. The word "Dreadnought" from a proper noun has become a common, significant of a class; and its meaning, as the generally adopted type of efficient battle-ship, is understood widely, if loosely. "Invincible" is undergoing a like modification. It means a battle-ship of Dreadnought proportions, but of inferior offensive and defensive powers, these qualities having been lessened in order to give much higher speed on the same tonnage. The type is essentially that known hitherto as the "armored cruiser." The United States does not contemplate Invincibles; rightly, as I believe, for I conceive the class to be a hybrid, with the drawbacks attributed to the crossing of species, that they combine the defects rather than the virtues of their progenitors. Still, Invincibles are undoubtedly formidable vessels, even if those be right who think them a mistake, as substitutes for an equivalent tonnage in Dreadnoughts. They are very much to be taken account of. The preponderance of German Dreadnoughts over American, 16 to 12, will be very seriously increased by the addition of five Invincibles.

These figures, however, are only to April 1st, 1914. The peculiarity of the German naval legislation is that, while dependent upon successive annual votes, it provides at one cast a programme for several future years. In consequence of this prevision, there can be, and is, coincident and harmonious progress in ship-construction, dockyard development, armaments, and ship-building plants. The great manufacturers know upon what to count, and can afford to spend on facilities money which they are assured they will get back in employment. The agitated question of one annual battle-ship, or two, or three, according to the various views of executive and legislature, in Great Britain or the United States, does not trouble the German employer of naval labor. The state is as much committed to its naval payments as the other countries are to the interest upon their debts.

The result has been, in Germany, a great increase not only of ships, but of power to build, both in quantity and in rapidity; so that it is a somewhat moot question whether Germany cannot, so far as facilities go, build as rapidly and as numerously as her richer rival. Great Britain can no longer surrender a start, as the hare did to the tortoise. Her immense programme of new construction for the year 1911 is due to the fact that, dallying some years ago with vague ideals of international agreements, she is now straining to recover the consequences of her nap, to regain a safe lead; for her security chiefly depends, not upon land forces to defend her soil against an enemy once on shore, but upon power to prevent his transit and his landing.

This suddenly and greatly increased programme, however, is not the only result of surrendering a sufficient superiority under a momentary impulse. Since the preceding words were written, in this current year, 1912, Great Britain, under the pressure of felt inadequacy of force in home waters, has modified dispositions of her fleet maintained for two centuries past; during which the Mediterranean, and British influences in it, have been considered essential factors in national security and in the European balance of power. The powerful battleship division known as the Atlantic fleet, stationed at Gibraltar, as a central point whence it would be equally available for use in the Mediterranean or in the Channel and North Sea, has been brought back to home waters; while the Mediterranean fleet, besides being weakened in numbers and strength, has been withdrawn from Malta to Gibraltar, leaving at the island only a division of cruisers. Independent of the military, and therefore political, significance of this measure, it is to be noted that almost one-half (49 per cent.) of British grain supplies now pass through the Mediterranean, three-fourths of which amount, being from the Black Sea, can come no other way. In such manner the present pays the negligence of the past. It is much as though the United States, by surrendering naval adequacy, should feel compelled in some future time to abandon the Caribbean.

In the course of the debate above cited, the British First Lord, replying to members of his own party, the Liberal, who objected to the proposed expenditures as exorbitant and unnecessary, said that if they intended to support a reduction, he would remind them of the fate of Aethelred the Unready; and he added, amid loud cheering, that a strong navy was a good foundation upon which to build up financial credit. This can only be by securing freedom from war, or, in case of war, the security for industry and commerce which a navy effects, thus ensuring the foundations of financial stability. Incidentally, the indemnities which have become a frequent incident of peace treaties are averted by the same precaution. The present annual expenditure of the United States upon the navy is one-eighth the war indemnity exacted from France by Germany after one year of hostilities, and one-fifth that which Japan endeavored to obtain from Russia. The motion to reduce was rejected in the British Parliament by 276 to 56—five to one.

The naval programme of Germany, when completed in 1920, will provide thirty-eight "capital" ships;[1] much the greater part of which will be of Dreadnought type, though probably some pre-Dreadnought vessels will still survive a few years longer. What is the significance of these conditions, in a state which up to a generation ago was non-naval?

Probably many reasons concur to one result. The industries and commerce, and not least the shipping trade, of Germany are in their present proportions a growth of thirty years, which has by no means reached its limit. All these elements of national prosperity depend upon free use of the sea; and the expansion of the navy results from the conviction that it must be so powerful that even Great Britain, menacing as her geographical situation is to Germany, and huge as is her fleet, will hesitate to withstand any policy on which Germany is set, will limit herself to her own protection, and to that of the colonies and interests which belong to her. This political situation is to be reinforced by a large development of the fleet of Austria-Hungary, opera-

[1] Since these words were written, the German Parliament, in May, 1912, has voted a further measure which will make the aggregate in 1920 to be 41 battle-ships. By the same enactment the *personnel* has been augmented by over 15,000 men, an increase of over 20 per cent. Great Britain now has avowedly abandoned the "two-power standard"—that is, that her navy should equal the combined numbers of any two other states,—and has announced that 60 per cent. over Germany alone is now her determination.

tive, as distinctly avowed, only in the Mediterranean, a principal line of British communications—imperial, colonial, and commercial. Here also increased national indebtedness is accepted deliberately, if anxiously. The number of Dreadnoughts proposed as the goal, by the Austrian Naval Secretary, is sixteen; of which four are in hand.

A century ago a very distinguished Swiss military writer, who saw much service throughout the Napoleonic period, who studied minutely many of the principal campaigns, and who reflected profoundly upon international relations as affecting war, and as affected by it, stated as a fundamental necessity of the European balance of power that no one state should be permitted to acquire an unchallengeable naval superiority. He had witnessed personally, and had appreciated, the decisive influence exerted over the whole conflict, continental as well as maritime, by the naval supremacy of Great Britain, and by the insular wealth consequent upon the naval shield extended over her commerce and industries. To-day the realization of his proposition is seen in the serious anxieties of Great Britain; challenged by a fleet, and by a possible combination of fleets, which, even though they may not together equal hers, may so endanger her superiority and her commerce as largely to limit her freedom of action in support of policies which otherwise may to her appear advisable, or even essential.

The proposition of a century ago related only to

Europe; but it has expanded, not by original forecast, but by inevitable growth, like the American Monroe Doctrine, so that it now fills the larger field of the world. The balances of power in Europe a hundred years since, constituted after the fall of Napoleon, were largely artificial, and consequently were not only complicated, but deficient in stability; because some of the larger units, the great powers, lacked homogeneity, or lacked completeness of territory, both which deficiencies are sources of unrest. In the intervening century progress has been made in eliminating these factors of discord. Austria has been separated from the greater part of Italy left under her control in 1815; and Italian unity has not only been consummated, but comprises almost all the territory racially and geographically Italian. Germany has achieved unity and expanded to limits which were by Bismarck considered commensurate to her claims and her needs. Austria, cut short in former ambitions in the direction of Italy, has made progress on the other side of the Adriatic. Although composed of elements proverbially discordant, she has held together for a time which gives promise of permanence. This is the more sure because the conditions are reinforced by a pressure on all sides, which necessitates the cohesion under one government of the various communities composing the empire, unless they wish to sink severally to the international insignificance which characterizes some of their Balkan neighbors.

These three great states, of comparatively recent origin as regards their present extent and constitution, and formally in alliance between themselves, are in a position to give effect to that challenge to British sea power which by the Swiss writer quoted was declared essential. And they are doing it. All parties in Great Britain except the so-called Labor party, which is distinctly *doctrinaire* in its views and policies, recognize that the question of national well-being is at stake; how much more the weight of Great Britain in the policies of the external world, in which a hundred years ago she occupied the decisive position. It is an odd circumstance that, at the very moment the Labor party in the British Parliament is opposing measures believed by most in the country necessary for national independence of action, the party of the same name in Australia, now controlling the government, defiantly announces that on certain points it will not admit arbitration, and that national defense is a prime element in its policy in order to insure national control of internal measures—that is, national independence.

These factors serve to link together in the appreciation of men the interrelation of the situation in Europe with the politics of the world. Great Britain cannot divest herself of responsibilities and policies external to the British Islands, except at the sacrifice of national interests and the acceptance of permanent degradation of national position. If the relative sea powers of Great Britain and of the three states of central Europe, which, if not opposed to her formally, nevertheless do stand in the opposite scale of the balance, were a matter of European international policies merely, the inhabitants of other continents might view the situation with unconcern, though with interest. But, in the infancy of Australian development, the dependence of Australia upon British control of the sea illustrates the far-reaching character of this element of European international relations.

If this were the only illustration, it might be relegated to the class of rare exceptions which fail to prove a rule; but it does not stand alone. Five years ago the sea power of Great Britain, by depriving Russia of naval allies, assured to Japan control of the sea. Can a similar effect continue to be exercised in view of the growing challenge to British naval supremacy? It is one thing to insure security of the British Islands against attack; it is quite another to be strong enough to insure national policy in matters of external effort.

A notable additional illustration is to be found in the Boer War of 1899–1901. The feeling of the Continent was with the Boers; it is useless now to recall the many manifestations of this bias, but the superiority of the British navy was such that interference was impossible. The result, superficially, was the overthrow of two small republics. Fundamentally, it secured the opportunity for several distinct and rival communities, in this respect somewhat resembling the Balkan States or those of Central America, to take a fresh start, and under the harmonizing influence of British political traditions to form a union such as that of the American thirteen colonies, or of the confederation which preceded the present German Empire.

This beneficial outcome is noteworthy; but the illustration of changed conditions of sea power is yet more impressive, because this localized disturbance in British imperial relations was precisely the kind of occurrence to which an empire so constituted is always liable, as in the case of the Indian mutiny of 1857. Standing alone, the British Islands may be able to defend their independence and commerce, to make an enemy ware of them; it is when called upon to repress disorder, or to oppose attack in some distant part of the empire, that the margin of naval superiority adequate to maintain peace or to protect the home country may prove insufficient. If so, the entire imperial system may break down. The possibility of such an embarrassment has always to be considered by Great Britain, when called upon to encounter a difficult international situation; and it is upon this calculation that Germany bases her expectation of controlling British political action by her own attitude of armed naval preparation. If disturbance actually occur, instead of remaining only contingent, the embarrassment evidently will be greater.

The forefront of this danger is unquestionably Germany. How far she is immediately the incentive to the proposed great increase of the Austrian navy to sixteen Dreadnoughts, or how far this measure is due to an Austrian determination to equal or surpass her ally, Italy, in control of their buffer sea, the Adriatic, it is impossible to say. Nor is it very necessary; for facts which can be seen, rather than purposes which can only be surmised, are the elements of power to be weighed and appreciated. The sympathies of nations fluctuate with their interests or with passing events, and their purposes vary accordingly. I remember when, in 1866, an American squadron was saluted in Chile as a savior. In 1891 the seamen of an American ship of war were mobbed through the streets of Valparaiso because of popular feeling excited against their nation. At the present moment an American ironclad is conveying to its final resting-place the dead body of a Chilean ex-President. It is not upon any ultimate designs of Germany that attention needs to fasten, but upon the indisputable fact that she will shortly possess a navy which in its aggregate none other than the British can withstand, and of which Great Britain herself must take grave account in all matters of external policy. The so-called Triple Entente is a recognition of this necessity. Already in one of its members, France, the question has arisen whether the battle-ship force, the solid infantry of the fleet, should not be concentrated in the Mediterranean, leaving to coast defenses and to the action of Great Britain, another member, the security of the Channel shores in case of a European war.

The question will naturally occur, How will these various conditions be affected by the formulation and acceptance of a treaty of arbitration between the United States and Great Britain, as advocated by Sir Edward Grey, covering every kind of differences, and rejecting explicitly every exception hitherto summed up under the words "vital interests and national honor"?

The reply is that no effect whatever is likely to be produced, except to intensify the resolution of Germany, unless the result upon popular opinion in the United States and Great Britain is such as to incline each of the contracting states to recognize the necessary international policies of the other, and to give support in case of need. Since the days of Bismarck, Germany frankly and explicitly avows the supremacy of force as the means of securing vital interests and of maintaining national honor. The comment of the German Chancellor of the Empire upon the report of Sir Edward Grey's speech explicitly confirms this statement. Such avowal involves necessarily, from the very habit of mind whence it springs, an appreciation of the limitations of force—what it can accomplish, and what it cannot. The consequence of this is diplomatic effort; combinations like those of a battle-field, albeit bloodless, based upon the recognition of common interests in the combining states, and also in great measure upon the elements of weakness or dissension in others. The result, as far as successful, is concentration on the one side, opposed to division on the other. Of these processes Bismarck in his day was a past master, nor does the hand of his successors seem wholly to have lost his cunning. The Triple Alliance, which he created, remains, after more than thirty years, one of the chief facts of international politics.

I should be unjust to Germany, and to my estimate of her reasonable national necessities and of her important international position, if I should not admit explicitly my conviction of the general correctness of her attitude in this respect. I do not hereby intimate any opinion upon particular actions; I speak only as a witness to general character as by me understood. I think, and have always thought, that the possession of force, of power, to effect ends is a responsibility—a talent, to use the Christian expression—which cannot by the individual man or state be devolved upon another, except when certain that the result cannot violate the individual or the national conscience. A general arbitration arrangement between Great Britain and the United States approaches this condition, because it is as certain as anything human can be that the two states will never again go to war, that their difficulties will always be settled peaceably. If there were no other reason, the interests and consequent sympathies of the British colonies, except perhaps those of Canada, would insure this.

It could be desired that differences between the two nations should be submitted, not to a third, outside, party, but to a commission composed of citizens of the two countries and of their colonies. Whether such a commission should be a Court, pronouncing upon a purely legal basis, may be doubted. There is an evident increasing indisposition to receive as convincing those decisions of courts which do not rest upon positive enactment but upon interpretation of law; upon inference and argument. Where there is a statute of clear yea and nay, submission may be given willingly; but there is less inclination to acquiesce in a course of deduction from stated legal premises to a conclusion in which popular prepossession is contradicted. This indisposition inevitably grows through the not infrequent occasions in which the highest courts have decided by a small majority of votes. Now in an international dispute there will be strong national prepossessions, and a court judgment depending upon so uncertain a basis as international law, interpreting and construing, is less likely to be acceptable than a decision by men of affairs which shall have the character of an adjustment, or compromise. A commission so constituted will be diplomatic rather than legal in character; but there seems no reason why the parties should not pledge acceptance of its decision as well as of that of a bench of judges.

Where differences are amenable to an existing law they can be referred to a tribunal of competent lawyers of whatsoever nationality; but in questions of policy, like the Monroe Doctrine, or the fortification of the Panama Canal before the Zone became United States territory, or the position of Great Britain in Egypt, or of Japan in Manchuria, determination does not concern lawyers as such, but men of affairs, because, there being no law applicable, what is needed is a workable arrangement based upon recognized conditions. Such arrangement becomes a law for the period of its duration.

This is precisely the situation in which Germany finds herself, and has found herself. The questions pressing upon her, though conditioned by law, have been and are questions of national policy and imminent national interests. The unification of the empire, the determination of its limits, the securing of conditions which should assure her weight in the councils of Europe, the extension of the sphere of German interests in the outside world, have been and are achievements of policy, accomplished against adverse conditions such as the United States and Great Britain have never known. To the effecting of them national power organized as military force has been and continues essential. Locked up in a territory narrow for its inhabitants, Germany must have an outlet for her industries secured by her own power, the only certain dependence. Her claims for such opportunity do not derive from law, and therefore, like many other questions, cannot in ultimate resort be settled by legal tribunals.

In conclusion, a word may be said upon the onerousness of armaments, so much insisted upon and so present to popular consciousness to-day. Undoubtedly, armaments are costly, but the means to bear them have increased to a degree little realized, if known at all.

In 1809 Great Britain was at the height of her single-handed struggle against Napoleon. During that year Austria was again crushed at Essling and Wagram. Prussia remained in the utter subjection to France to which Jena, Eylau, and Friedland had reduced her in 1806 and 1807. Russia was the ally of France. The Spanish peninsula was flooded with French armies; a French King ruled in Madrid, another in Holland, while the royal family of Portugal was fugitive in Brazil. The Peninsular War was still in its beginnings, but in full blast. During that year the revenue collected in the United Kingdom was £63,719,400, supplemented by loans to the amount of £12,298,379; total, £76,017,779. The total expenditure was £76,566,013, of which the actual current expenses were £52,352,146; the remainder being interest upon the debt. Of the current expenses the military and naval were £48,210,957. The trade of the kingdom during this year, export and import together, amounted to £91,872,308. Excluding Ireland, the population in 1811, a census year, was 12,596,803.

33

A hundred years later, in 1909, the revenue collected was £151,578,295. The expenditure was £152,292,395, of which £59,028,000 was for army and navy. The trade, export and import, amounted to £1,094,485,426. The population, again excluding Ireland,[1] was 40,634,263. That is, with little more than thrice the population of 1809, there is nearly twelve times the commerce, or four times as much per head; and while the total expenditure has doubled, increased by one hundred per cent., that for army and navy at this present period of gigantic armaments has increased by less than one-fourth, by less than twenty-five per cent.

It may be urged that the expenditure of 1809 was for actual war, which involves a disproportionate additional outlay over that of armament in peace. True; but this merely means that it costs much less to be ready for war than to go to war—another way of regarding Washington's maxim that preparation for war is the best assurance of peace. The thing to be observed is that, with an increase of nearly three hundred per cent. of trade in proportion to population, there is only twenty-five per cent. increase in military expenditure. The increase of revenue collected approached one hundred and fifty per cent. in 1909, and has since exceeded that mark.

These considerations are not advanced in order to contest that armament is a burden. They show

[1] Ireland is excluded in both cases because, though I have found its population stated for 1909, I have not for the earlier year.

only that the burden is not unbearable in itself, because it is very much less than has been borne. If it tends to internal revolt and to the breakdown of civilization, as Sir Edward Grey affirmed, it will not be because men cannot endure it, but because they will not.

The question for civilized men is whether, under all the world-wide conditions confronting this era, restiveness under the burden is a sign of progress or of decay.

II

DIPLOMACY AND ARBITRATION

NOT long ago I was the guest of a large club in New York devoted to economical subjects and interests, and was an attentive listener to several speeches which found their common inspiration in the belief that arbitration could be substituted for war in all cases. It was apparent throughout that by arbitration was meant judicial arbitration, the decision of a court based upon a code of accepted law, not merely an arrangement of differences by adjustment or compromise contrived by practical men of affairs dealing with a difficult situation. Such adjustments have marked hitherto almost all treaties or settlements of any character between disputing nations, and they come under the head of diplomacy. It appeared to be granted that such codified law does not exist yet, but its possibility in the future was assumed by the generality of the speakers. "Law in place of War" voiced the aspiration of one; but it is scarcely a misrepresentation to say that effectually law instead of diplomacy was the desired end. For in diplomacy, in international negotiation, force underlies every contention as a possible final arbiter, and of force war is simply the ultimate expression.

The audience was necessarily sympathetic. The economist as such, and as a rule, cannot but hate war with a peculiar and specific hatred. Its occurrence throws his favorite system into disorder, dislocates the gearing; and the preparations for war are of the nature of so-called unproductive labor in various forms. Independent of the humanitarian evils of actual war which no soldier, not even the most zealous, will deny nor fail to deplore, preparation for war diverts an army of producers for a fixed period of their lives from productive labor, usually so styled, to military training, as well as another subordinate big detachment of work-people to the manufacture of weapons of war. The creation of these, from an industrial point of view, is labor wasted, because spent in producing materials economically useless for purposes economically deplorable; at least to a first glance. It may be suggested here, however, as I have on other occasions, that the recognized financial priority and supremacy of Great Britain during the greater part of the last century was really the result of the armed power, the so-called unproductive labor, which through more than a century shielded her industries and commerce. From this point of view, the debt incurred and the power expended were of the nature of an investment, in which, as in many other investments, the investor is content to wait through an unremunerative period for the great returns of a discernible. future.

A listener who had reached his threescore and ten, whose life had been passed, and his position in life determined, by devotion to pursuits so contrary to the mind of his fellow-diners—a military man, in short—could scarcely at the age named listen without a certain element of doubt, of lingering over the past; or without a certain repugnance and dissent to denunciations and prophecies which, if just, signified the passing away of a profession with which his life had been identified, and in the heroes of which he had had occasion to notice, and to know, the elements of greatness which exalted their calling. A member of the First Hague Conference, and an interested observer of international affairs for years back, I have become conscious, and seek to bear ever in mind that professional prepossession cannot but constitute in me a bias, against which I must be continually on guard, in viewing the origin and progress of the various attempts to substitute other processes for the attainment of the objects which hitherto have been effected largely by war; the study of which, with the consequent absorption of military sympathies, has been the principal engagement of my life experience.

Nevertheless, while thus keeping guard over the temper of my mind, and recognizing that to prefer a state of war to a state of peace would be a grievous twist of character, I could not but think that in the speeches to which I listened there were to be detected fallacies, partial points of view, ignoring of difficult factors. Fundamental among these was the looking upon war as a principal rather than an agent; as a cause rather than an effect. There was no explicit recognition of the fact that force, under one form or another, underlies law itself; and that there are necessities which transcend law, a truth which found expression in the phrase once familiar to American ears—"a higher law." There was also the assumption that the individual man has surrendered unreservedly his freedom of action to the commands of law. I long ago pointed out that this is not true. The Fugitive Slave Law afforded an instance. American citizens of the most law-abiding and peaceful character in other matters simply refused in this to subject their conscience to law. The instance is too recent to be dismissed as out of date, as some perhaps may feel can be done with the long history of religious persecution, and of the martyrs to opinion who refused therein to subject their consciences to law. Armed resistance—that is, war— helped to win for mankind freedom of conscience.

At the present moment our own United States, through its cherished Monroe Doctrine, refuses directly, as it has refused for generations, to acquiesce in a procedure which according to the law of nations is strictly legal. The refusal is not based on grounds of conscience, moral grounds, but on dictates of expediency; a justifiable motive, but one which rests on a distinctly lower plane. Sir Harry Johnston, a distinguished British administrator of long service in Africa, who may be better known to many Americans by his recent book, *The Negro in America*, contributed to the *Nineteenth Century*, in December, 1910, and January, 1911, two successive articles designed to explain to Englishmen the feelings of Germany. By this exhibition of "the other side" he avowedly hoped to forward, if possible, a good understanding, in place of the mutual suspicion now characterizing the attitude of the two nations, which finds expression in the generally known naval ship-building competition. The views he put forth depend upon personal discussions "with German officials, politicians, men of science, heads of industries, and of great commercial firms." In fact, his first article is couched in terms of German opinion expressing itself, and, as such, is embraced in quotation-marks.

In the course of the long exposition of the grievances felt by Germany, and of her sense of being, as it were, "in Coventry," politically, occur these words:

Why, Germans ask, in and as regards America, should everything be settled now practically by a joint understanding between Britain and the United States? Why was Denmark some time ago forbidden to sell one or more West-Indian Islands to the Germans as a depot for their fleet in the New World? France, Holland, and Denmark, as well as the British and American Empires, have harbors, coaling-stations, and colonies in the New World, which, especially in the tropical portions, serve as valuable rendezvous for their commerce; why should it be tacitly laid down that if Germany by purchase attempted to get a coaling-station, or a harbor of refuge, it would be equivalent to a *casus belli* with the Anglo-Saxon world?

In his second article,[1] elicited by the number of letters and remonstrances consequent upon the first, the writer endeavors to attenuate the impression produced by these words; but expressions once given public vogue are with difficulty recalled, and in this instance, while facts remain vague, there is left no room for doubt as to feelings:

No German ever mentioned to me any project entertained by Germans for acquiring an island in the West Indies. It is true that some Germans, in their review of recent history, consider it to have been unfair and churlish on the part of the United States, and perhaps of Great Britain, to have opposed the project of the sale of a Danish island to Germany; but the subject was dismissed as one of only academic interest.

Whether this transaction of sale and purchase between Denmark and Germany was actually undertaken and forbidden, and, if so, by whom, I have no means of knowing; but, like every other American, I do know that it would have been contrary to the Monroe Doctrine, which is a distinct, continuous, and developing policy of the United States through now nearly three generations—since long before the present German Empire was constituted. But a policy, however wise or imperative to national interests, as I believe the Monroe Doctrine to have

[1] *Nineteenth Century*, January, 1911, p. 83

been in origin and in development, is not a law. Consider the proposition as formulated by Sir Harry Johnston's article quoted. The sovereign and independent State of Denmark proposes to sell a piece of national property to the equally sovereign and independent Empire of Germany. What is there in international law to forbid? And if nothing, what is there to make the transaction illegal? In the existing condition of international law—by which an arbitral court must be governed—how is the suggested transfer to be condemned, or denied, if brought to a judicial arbitrament? Yet that which such a court must concede, so far as I can see, the United States refuses to concede, and in my own opinion very rightly.

This is one instance of the difficulty which I foresee, an insurmountable difficulty, to the substitution of judicial arbitration for diplomacy in all cases. The insistence of the United States and the tacit, if unwilling, acquiescence of Germany are both matters of policy. That of the United States is generally understood; that of Germany is not avowed, for it is not a general policy, only a particular abstinence. Germany has never explicitly recognized the Monroe Doctrine as an element in her general policy, as Great Britain very recently has done publicly, by the mouth of a responsible representative of her government, Sir Edward Grey, the Secretary for Foreign Affairs in the present cabinet. His words were: "The Americans have a policy associated with the name of Monroe, the cardinal point of which is that no European or non-American nation should acquire fresh territory on the continent of America. If it be, as I think it must be, a postulate of any successful arbitration treaty of an extended kind that there should be no conflict, or possibility of conflict, between the national policies of the nations who are parties to it, this condition is assumed between us." [1] Coming at the moment it did, the statement suggests the undercurrent of exchange of views which necessarily accompanied the negotiation of the then pending Anglo-American Arbitration Treaty, subsequently arranged by the two governments, but fundamentally modified by the American Senate.

As far as has transpired, the official attitude of Germany toward the Monroe Doctrine leaves nothing to be desired by Americans, but she has never made, to my knowledge, a distinct pronouncement in its support such as the above. Speaking under correction, it appears to me that if the question posed in Sir Harry Johnston's article were raised under an unqualified treaty of arbitration with Germany, and it went so before a court, the United States would lose its case, and must accept a German naval station in the waters of the Caribbean Sea, with all consequences. Among these consequences, we may be assured by the sensible adequacy of all German military action, would be the impregnable

[1] *The Spectator*, May 27, 1911.

fortification of the station. A fortified German base in the West Indies would greatly complicate for us the strategic, and therefore the diplomatic, situation in the Caribbean Sea, and at the Panama Canal. The first effect would be additional fortification of the principal French and British positions; the ultimate result the transference of a European war between these powers, such as threatened in 1911, to American waters—one of the very contingencies which the Monroe Doctrine seeks to avert. Let us note the precedent of Helgoland. Ceded to Germany by Great Britain in 1890, it is now a formidably fortified advanced torpedo base, which must seriously condition all movements of a British fleet in the North Sea. Such an acquisition is an instance of naval strategy operating in peace.

A conviction of similar character with reference to the legal merits of our contention with Spain in 1898 was expressed to me, when a delegate to the Hague Conference in 1899, by the principal representative of one of the smaller European Powers. The Spanish War itself affords an instance in which arbitration was avoided, and diplomacy settled once for all a long-vexed question by ultimate resort to force—to armaments. The person in question was a man of mature age who had passed his life in diplomacy, much of it in the United States, where he had married an American woman. He was then minister for his country to one of the principal European states, which may be taken to indicate his standing with his own government. Our demands upon Spain at that time and our course of action could not be justified in law, he thought, before an international court deciding between the two countries. Our demands, as phrased in the joint resolution of Congress, were based upon "the abhorrent conditions which for more than three years had existed in the island of Cuba, so near our own borders." The incident of the *Maine* was mentioned, but it was supplementary and cumulative—cited as incidental to the general conditions, not as a primary cause of action. This is a fact well to be kept in mind at this particular moment.[1] In other words, the domestic conditions of a certain integral portion of the Spanish Empire were given as the motive of the demand which led to war; precisely as the domestic institution of slavery, though not the immediate motive to the War of Secession, had led by a series of inevitable consequences to conditions which caused war.

International law concedes the legal right of any state to declare war, leaving it arbiter of its own action. It does not concede the like right of one independent state to intervene in the domestic concerns of another, except by permission or at the price of war. It is easy to see that such right of

[1] The allusion here was to the prospective raising of the *Maine*, then (May, 1911) in process of preparation. If the exposed hull had shown signs that the origin of the explosions was internal, the cry would have been uttered at once that the United States had gone to war in excitement over a mistake.

intervention would be contrary to the sovereignty of the state. Although self-government is not necessarily equivalent to independence—Spain proposed autonomy for Cuba as an ultimate solution, but refused to entertain the proposition of independence —independence includes self-government. Foreign intervention in domestic concerns impeaches both, whether such intervention be by another state or by an exterior tribunal. The demand of the United States that Spain should evacuate Cuba, leaving its people free and independent, could not, therefore, be justified by law if brought before a tribunal, unless Spain were willing to submit to the Court the question of whether she should remain in Cuba or not; a precedent which, if established, might carry us far, and bring into litigation much of the existing status of the world.

Yet, consider the moral grounds for forcible intervention; concerning which a distinguished British officer, who, it happens, by a rarity among British soldiers, is a strong Liberal in politics, said to me, "If the conditions of Cuba had existed as close to our doors as to those of the United States, we would have interfered similarly." Since then—I like to vouch for my authorities—the officer in question has occupied continuously higher and higher positions in the civil and military administration of his government. Mr. John Hay, the American Ambassador at London, during the months immediately preceding the war, affirmed at the time this general attitude in England. "The commonest phrase here is: 'I wish you would take Cuba at once. We wouldn't have stood it this long.'" Consider, I repeat, the conditions. In 1900 a very prominent gentleman, whose name, if mentioned, would be recognized by three-fourths of those who may read these lines and who had had close observation of Cuba during the revolt, said to me: "I asked Senator Proctor why, in the report of his visit to Cuba, he had not mentioned such-and-such things. The reply was, 'If I had told all I saw, there would have been no holding our people back'"; and at the moment there were still hopes of a peaceful solution. I may add I have verified this recollection by a present reference to my informant.

If the hand of the United States had been stayed in this instance by an adverse arbitral decision upon legal grounds, upon what other legal grounds could the Court have proceeded to right the misgovernment, to which was due the hopeless sufferings endured by the innocent Cuban population? Hopeless, I say, for it may be considered demonstrated that Spain, with the best intentions, has not the political aptitudes for well-governing remote dependencies. All that could come before an International Arbitral Court was the case between the United States and Spain. Spain's dealing with the revolt was a matter of domestic policy, not under the jurisdiction of a court instituted to decide international questions only. As it was, diplomacy

47

settled that to which law was incompetent. It did so by using its last argument—force. It is out of place here to enlarge upon the benefits that American occupation, the result of war, conferred upon the ceded colonies of Spain. ⊸Sir Harry Johnston, in one of the articles already cited, says, quite incidentally:

> To what degree have not the Santo Domingans, Porto Ricans, Cubans, and Filipinos profited through the intervention of the United States? I can testify from personal observation of the first three that the only adverb to be used in this connection is "enormously."

Yet the intervention, if my diplomatic friend was right, could not have been permitted by a tribunal of arbitration. Such can decide only upon positive law, or upon fair rational inference from some existing law, or precedent, applied to a novel condition; in such case a legal inference rather than a positive law. There is as yet no proposition to constitute a tribunal empowered to authorize intervention in the domestic affairs of an independent state, or itself to exercise such intervention; but it seems probable that, in the borderland where international and domestic meet, there may be found the means of a transition to such interference. If so, this will trench heavily on that principle of nationality which has been the distinguishing element in modern European progress ever since the centralizing conception of the Roman Empire and the strong intervening hand of the Papal arbiter lost their hold on European mankind.

The vista opened by such a prospect is indeed formidable, yet already there are premonitions of the attempt. At the International Peace Conference held in Stockholm in August, 1910, a native Egyptian asked the conference to express its sympathy with the Nationalist cause in Egypt, and to direct that the Egyptian question should be placed on the programme of the next conference. Instead of laying the proposal aside, as being under present conditions not an international question, the Congress decided to leave the matter to the Peace Bureau at Berne. A similar course would doubtless have been taken if a Filipino had requested a like interference for the Philippines; and the fact that a small but active minority in the United States would have sustained the proposition shows the greater chance there is that an Arbitral International Court might thus extend its jurisdiction by unconscious usurpation. It is easy to see that questions such as this approach a border-line which might be insensibly crossed. There are questions of domestic regulation which affect foreign states, possibly unequally and invidiously. At present, the time-honored custom of nations is to respect the national sovereignty, confining objection to diplomatic remonstrance; or, if the worst come, resorting to war, which does not infringe national sovereignty. It seems likely enough, however, that, once familiarized by habit with the idea of external intervention, such questions as the regulation of immigration, as a matter

of intercourse between nations, might be brought
before an arbitral court. Our government has not
thought necessary to ask the consent of other nations to fortifying the Panama Canal; but in influential quarters in Germany and Great·Britain
it has been suggested that to arbitrate this question,
which affects "the vital interests of a great nation,"
would be highly edifying.

At the First Hague Conference there were audible
whispers of two skeletons in the closet of the International Happy Family there assembled which might
at any moment be revealed. As is the case with all
such skeletons, unless they do appear, mention was
reserved and vague; but there can be little doubt
that they were there, though kept throughout
decently curtained. They each illustrate questions
in which legal decisions would probably be a far
less happy solution than that of the rude hand of
power. Moreover, they were on that borderland of
international and domestic where intrusion by an
external power needs to be most jealously watched;
because it will tend by gradual precedent to broaden
the scope of arbitration at the expense of the principle of national self-government involved in national independence. Of these questions one was
the desire of the Papacy to be admitted to representation in the Conference; and a somewhat curious
incident attending its close was the reading to the
assembled members an admonition addressed, if
I rightly remember, to the Dutch government, as

the formal convener of the conference, commenting on the absurdity of excluding from a peace conference the Power which it was claimed had done so much to advance the cause of peace in the world.

The conference being an assembly of secular states, not spiritual, the admission of a papal representative could only be as that of a temporal power, to which, it was said, Italy demurred; and naturally, because it would have recognized the temporal power which the Papacy still claimed as against the Italian occupation. Yet, why was the Papacy not a temporal power, legally, in 1899? It claims to be so in its own right unsurrendered, despite the Italian occupation, which from the papal point of view did not alter the legal fact; just as the United States dates its independence from its own declaration, not from recognition by Great Britain. The essence of a state—as the word shows—is that it exists by its own will. The only thing, as yet, that can reverse that will is the accepted result of force. International law accepts accomplished facts. The secular occupation of Rome, which the world at large, outside of the devout adherents of the Papacy, justifies as morally right, is now legally complete and, therefore, is now such a fact; but, however morally right, it could never have been accomplished by arbitration. The Papacy would probably have refused to arbitrate, to acknowledge any superior judge in its own case; but, if brought to court at the first, the facts would have been that the Papacy then was a secular government of long standing, *de jure* and *de facto*, and no counsel of expediency could have swerved a just court from the decision that it had all the legal qualifications entitling it to continue. Italy would have been maimed of its capital.

The other skeleton was the dispute between the British government and the Boer Republics. These —it was scarcely a secret, even open—were trying hard to get the matter before the conference, in the shape, probably, of admitting delegates. This step would have acknowledged as unqualified an independence which in British affirmation was qualified, and at most amounted to the right of self-government. Sovereignty, which is the attribute of a state wholly independent, was in their case qualified by the unrelinquished suzerainty of Great Britain. If this were so, and, after careful reading of the official papers at the time, I think it certainly was, any recognition of the republics, or cognizance of the dispute, would have been an intrusion into the domestic affairs of Great Britain, just as any question by another state of our administration of the Philippines would be. The Philippines, however useful our occupation may be to the inhabitants, are ours by right of conquest from Spain, by legal right; and our administration there is a purely domestic concern.

At the time, as I read the agreements between Great Britain and the Boer Republics by which their relations were then determined, Great Britain had not any right, and expressly disclaimed any right, to interfere with their self-government, including the question of the suffrage, on which most hinged; no right, that is, except the right of war, which as yet belongs to every state which feels it has wrongs to be redressed. If recourse to war by Great Britain were excluded, through consenting to judicial arbitration, no redress by law was possible to the internal abuses of a government concerning which Mr. Bryce, an opponent of the war, wrote:

President Krüger and his advisers committed the fatal mistake of trying to maintain a government which was at the same time undemocratic and incompetent. An exclusive government may be pardoned, if it is efficient; an inefficient government, if it rests upon the people. But a government which is both inefficient and exclusive incurs a weight of odium under which it must ultimately sink, and this was the kind of government which the Transvaal attempted to maintain.

Yet, despite this severe condemnation by an observer who at the worst was unbiased, a court could have given no redress, because the legal facts were against it; that is, the legal fact of the right to self-government conceded in a convention by Great Britain. The result, under the international law of then and now, was war, and consequent upon war such a political reconstitution as has replaced a congeries of rival and partly hostile communities, with strong racial oppositions, by a union of states. A South-African of English birth, who has resided

53

there since the war and been active in politics, told me recently that in his judgment nothing but union could have saved another war. Union would have been impossible under the old conditions of Boer self-government in two states; and only force could have solved a difficulty to which existing international law was incompetent.

At the dinner in question much stress was laid by one of the speakers upon the opinion expressed to him by a well-known president of an American university, that all the wars in which the United States has been involved since that of independence could have been avoided. This is one of those remarks which says either too little or too much. If it is meant that in each instance, if both parties had been reasonable and righteous in their acts, there need not have been war, too little was said. No one will dispute the assertion so qualified. If it is meant that, things being as they actually were, war could have been avoided, too much is affirmed. Doubtless opinions may differ, and this may be considered matter of opinion, but as such it may be discussed.

Of the Mexican War I have no competent knowledge; but I am familiar with the War of 1812, with the conflict of views and interests which led to the War of Secession, and to a somewhat less degree with the causes of the War with Spain. If it is meant that an arbitral court could have settled these disputes upon legal grounds, the reply is that, in one of the two principal causes which led to the War of 1812,

Great Britain, while maintaining the necessity and consequent propriety of its action, admitted it to be without sanction in law. An arbitral court could have affirmed no more. In 1861 a like arbitration, whatever its result in conceding or denying the right of secession, would have maintained slavery in existence for generations longer, for the United States government did not allege slavery as a justification of the war; a course which alienated many warm foreign sympathizers. Abolition was a war measure pure and simple. It could never have been a result of legal arbitration.

In the War with Spain there were no legal grounds upon which an arbitral court could have decreed the relinquishment by Spain of her colonies. War alone—actual or threatened—could have enforced the demand of the United States that Cuba be evacuated, and from war resulted the beneficent progresses that are known and noted. It is not claimed here that these subsequent benefits, even could they have been certainly anticipated, would justify a recourse to war. They might, or they might not. Every such case must be determined on its own merits; but, as a rule, it is not advantage to be gained, but wrong to be redressed, which justifies war. As a matter of private opinion, the members of a court of arbitration might have considered it demonstrated that the time for Spain to go had fully come; but as a matter of legal decision there was then, and is now, no ground upon which to base a judicial sentence to that effect. Diplomacy failing, war alone was competent, and war alone still would be. I am aware that persons in eminent position believed that with delay all the results of the war could have been secured from the Spanish government without bloodshed. Granting that they were not mistaken, the difference of agency would have been that between war potential and war actual; in either case force, intimated by the United States, would have determined the issue. The ground of domestic bad government, however extreme, is not one for an international court; exactly as the ground of good government does not constitute the legal justification of the presence of Great Britain in Egypt or of the United States in the Philippines, however deplorable might be the results of withdrawal in either case.

III

NAVIES AS INTERNATIONAL FACTORS

In the first article of this series I have mentioned the purpose of the German government concerning the scope and development of its naval policy and the numbers of the fleet commensurate with that policy. This purpose was formulated in a law which as first passed, in 1900, was operative over a term of many years then, and to some extent now still future. The principle underlying was expressed in a preamble which stated that it was essential to possess a navy of such force that to incur hostilities with it would jeopardize the supremacy of the greatest naval power—a parliamentary way of designating Great Britain without the personality of mentioning a name.

Upon this principle, which may be defined as that of securing national peace, coupled with power to take at any time such international action as the policy of the moment might dictate, the constitution and numbers of the prospective German fleet were decided. Germany has abounded in assurances that the progress of her navy from year to year has no reference to the current ship-building programme of Great Britain. This statement is doubtless literally true; and is to be reconciled with the preamble above quoted by the fact that, having then considered the present and probable future of British naval development, and the wide-spread naval and colonial responsibilities of the British Empire, it was possible to reach a very close approximation to the numbers and character of the vessels needed to meet the requirements of the German policy avowed. It has been noted that in this calculation an important element has been the liability of Great Britain to be distracted and embarrassed at critical moments, of negotiation or of war, by disturbances or attacks involving distant transmarine dominions. This may impose either a diminution of naval force in home waters or the abandonment to itself of the remote dependency. To such peril Germany is far less exposed. As a matter of fact, the result has been that the standard of British naval construction has been set in Germany, not that of German construction in Great Britain, except in the original design.

It is not necessary to know the precise reasoning by which the responsible German authorities reached the exact constitution and numbers laid down by them as corresponding to the principle. The reasoning may have been faulty, the conclusion erroneous— inadequate or exaggerated. Indeed, that it was imperfect is testified by some subsequent amendments, not many, known as *novelle*. One of the most important of these has been enacted a year after this paper was first written. It increased the proposed ultimate strength of the battle-fleet in 1920 from thirty-eight to forty-one; while the personnel is augmented by fifteen thousand—over twenty per cent. The number of ships in active commission in home waters, and consequently of officers and crews in constant readiness, is considerably enlarged, while no change is made in the number of vessels in foreign service. The international significance of all this is obvious. Modification is inherent in all designs which have in them a principle of life, and in this the German scheme has illustrated the common lot; but the comprehensive precision of the principle, combined with the particular feature of legislative expenditure predetermined for many years, which is alien to American and British theory, have preserved consistency and harmony of action. In this the German result contrasts strongly with the fits and starts characteristic of government by party, of annual appropriations unenlightened by any continuous definiteness of scheme, in which regard to the votes of the voters takes precedence of regard to the interests of the voters—that is, of the nation.

I guard myself, of course, from expressing any serious dissent from the method of the United States and of Great Britain, in annual appropriations controlled by the legislature of each successive year. It is in accord with the genius of their institutions, and therefore best suited to their practice; while it possesses the incontestable merit of preserving the guardianship of the purse which is the foundation of their edifice of liberty. In short, it is consistent with their whole scheme of government; while the drawback, that expenditures are viewed not with a single eye to national needs, but with a double regard to that and to the next election, is equally characteristic and perhaps equally essential to government by the people.

The difference between this method and the German is that which naturally exists between governments where the executive preponderates and that where the legislature does; and the result accordingly is greater executive efficiency in the one and less in the other. Representative Germans deprecate government by party. Experience shows that they are right, so far as executive results are concerned; and it is an important question for consideration whether, in the present tendency of the world, executive efficiency is not about to become the most essential attribute of government. More and more, in our individualistic scheme of popular government, we are feeling, and legislation is showing, the need of governmental—that is, of executive—control. That such control depends upon legislation does not invalidate the fact that in exercise it is an executive function.

The unsteadiness of naval policy dependent upon party government has received recent conspicuous illustration in Great Britain, the country which most of all depends upon naval efficiency. The particular feature of British government—that the Executive is a commission chosen from the legislature, thus qualifying the opposition of idea between executive and legislative functions—has not prevented the policy of a party, appealing for popular support, from bidding for such support by economies real or apparent; the reaction from which, itself the reflection of popular alarm, is found in a one year's sudden immense increase of expenditure. In our own government, where legislature and executive, though co-ordinate, are distinct in person as in function, each must lean naturally to the support of the functions which are intrusted to it. The executive cannot but desire means fully adequate to the duties laid upon it; it will tend to err, if at all, by excess of demand in this direction. The legislature, controlling the expenditure, and responsible for its provision, will tend naturally to contest the executive estimates, even though it may be itself extravagant in other directions, for reasons more or less open to criticism.

Taking Germany and Great Britain for momentary comparison in respect of effective co-operation between executive and legislature, it may justly be said that the former illustrates a measured, graduated progress, dependent upon principle, and upon calculation based on principle; whereas the other, while certainly not without a general conviction of the need of naval supremacy, which does rough duty as a principle, does not possess that definiteness of conception which results in a fixed and calculated policy. The "two-power standard" and "the two keels for one"—that is, two ships laid down for Germany's one—are phrases with a meaning; but, although the former is in essence more than a century old, neither represents a process of reasoning. They are simply snap judgments; not the outcome of mental consideration, acting upon known factors deliberately weighed and measured. The advantage of the German method has received high indorsement from eminent British authority. Sir William White, for nearly twenty years chief constructor of the British navy, writes in the *Atlantic Monthly* of August, 1911, "Efficient and economical administration of any navy can be achieved only when *annual estimates form part of a complete scheme*, embracing the creation and maintenance of a warfleet adequate for the defense of the country to which it belongs. That scheme may be modified from time to time, but it should be always in existence."

The German principle—I speak of the principle only, neither criticizing nor indorsing the calculations based upon it—possesses among other merits the very great one of asserting with absolute clearness that the constitution and numbers of a navy are not a matter of domestic policy, but of foreign relations. I lay stress upon this because I conceive, and further on shall attempt to show, that failure clearly to recognize this is the fundamental defect in naval policy as realized in the United States. This underlies the battledore-and-shuttlecock contest, of one, or two, or more, annual battle-ships, played between executive and legislature, or between opposing parties in the legislature. Germany, says the declaration above quoted, needs a navy of such strength that the greatest naval power will not lightly incur hostilities. That certainly is a purely international consideration. It has nothing to do with German domestic affairs, except to indicate their dependence upon international security based upon armed force. It does not mean that Germany wants to fight Great Britain; even less that she imagines that in 1914 with sixteen Dreadnoughts she can successfully meet the British twenty-two, if these be concentrated. What it means is that if Germany wishes to carry a point of foreign policy to which Great Britain objects—and their interests are markedly contrary in several quarters—Great Britain, despite her superior fleet, will think more than twice before her resistance takes the ultimate form of force, because that may mean war; and in war, if some of her distant interests are endangered, as for instance in the Mediterranean or India or Australia, her fleet, though superior, cannot spare necessary detachments to those threatened points, because of the requirement to be always superior to Germany in northern Europe.

Men readily imagine that there has been no war

·when there has been no bloodshed, no fighting. War in modern conception and practice is business, not fighting. It is carrying a point through the opponent's sense of inability to resist. The less the fighting, the better, the business; just as in a campaign of actual war the manoeuvering which attains a result without fighting, by strategic dispositions placing a superior force in a point of decisive vantage, is more creditable than the bloodiest of head-on victories. Two hundred years ago a great French admiral said, "The best victories are those which cost least in blood, hemp, and iron"—in life and in material.

These thoughts should be commonplaces; but they are not, because they are not common to most men. Austria, as a matter of international policy, three years ago assumed by force full sovereignty over Bosnia and Herzegovina. It was a lawless act, in that it disregarded a treaty which was part of the public law of Europe; but it was justifiable, because it was evident that if in the Turkish revolution the Young Turks obtained control—as they have—they would have contested the conclusion. Under the new conditions the continued existence of Turkish suzerainty over the two provinces would involve international friction, just as Turkish suzerainty over Crete, an empty yet vexatious political fact, has caused and is still causing much trouble and is pregnant of more. Turkey's recent purchase of two out-of-date German battle-ships is meant primarily to insure that Crete shall not go the way of her Balkan provinces.

The annexation by Austria was a change of political relation rather than of actual tenure; but all the same it was an act of war. When Russia and Great Britain showed resentment, and France discontent, Germany threw her sword into the balance. It would have been heavier if her fleet had progressed further, but it was heavy enough. There was again war, but no bloodshed. Results were accomplished; but by force, however disguised. Bulgaria seized the same opportunity to cast off the Turkish suzerainty. Again force, war in all but striking; but Bulgaria was armed. Unlucky Greece and still more unhappy Crete were caught unprepared, or else were controlled successfully by the Western Powers, so that the same opportunity slipped away from them unimproved. The most appealing and rightful of all political motives, the desire of two kindred and neighboring communities to come under one government, and of one of them to escape an alien bond, is denied; and they themselves have cause for regret that the hour found them unprepared. This very unreadiness is possibly the best justification for the continuance of that force which retains the Cretans still the nominal subjects of Turkey.

These instances have a special interest because they illustrate both why nations use force, and how law is incapable of meeting difficulties which force solves; not only easily, but finally and for the best. By law Bosnia and Herzegovina belonged to Turkey, but were in Austrian occupation. It was expedient beyond question that the tenant should become the owner; but what law can be evoked to compel the transfer? Diplomacy may arrange; a tribunal can only decide. The change of Bulgaria to an independent from a tributary state was equally a transfer of ownership; beyond law, though not beyond diplomacy, nor the force which is an expression of diplomatic factors. The continued dependence of Crete upon Turkey, instead of her desired incorporation with Greece, is the maintenance of a lawful ownership. No judge can reverse the facts or construe otherwise the law; but before the higher law of the reasonable wishes of the people affected, it is a blatant iniquity.

More almost than armies, which in these changes were the instruments of forcible yet beneficent adjustments, navies are instruments of international relations. They are so more purely, because a navy, as has long been recognized, can very rarely be used to oppress the people of its country in their domestic conditions, as armies often have been. While thus more strictly international, the scope of navies is also far wider. They can be felt where the national armies cannot go, except under naval protection. Just here it becomes necessary to point out a further distinction, which closely affects the United States and shows more clearly how entirely the navy, and consequently the numbers and constitution of the navy, is a matter to be determined by international considerations, and not merely by those which are domestic and internal to the country. Exactly as a navy cannot be used as an instrument of domestic oppression, so in international affairs it is less effective for aggression than armies are; yet to a state whose frontiers are maritime, and to the external interests of such a state, it is more effective as a defensive force for protection, because of its mobility. The United States has neither the tradition nor the design to act aggressively beyond seas, but she has very important transmarine interests which need protection, as well as two home coasts separated by a great intervening space and open to attack.

The question for the United States, as regards the size of its navy, is not so much what it desires to accomplish as what it is willing or not willing to concede. For instance, we have shown plainly that we are unwilling to concede anything as regards the control of the Panama Canal, even to discuss the right to fortify it. The Monroe Doctrine, too, is only a claim to maintain security for that which we possess. In no sense does it propose to add to our holdings. How far is the country prepared to be obliged to concede on these points, because unready to maintain them by organized force?

It is upon such general considerations that the naval policy of a nation should be constituted.

But the snare which the proverb asserts to lie in generalities must be recognized. A principle is essentially a generality. It is in the application of it to a concrete case that the difficulty lies. In that before us, the constitution and numbers of the necessary fleet is the result, to be sought by the application of the principle to the national conditions. Thus may be reached a defined and accepted policy, which, though lacking the regulated provision for a somewhat distant future which German institutions permit and have formulated, will nevertheless exercise over legislation a control that in result will be similar. The state will not contract a definite obligation to be fulfilled by successive legislatures, bound as by the interest of a debt, as Germany has done; but a definite standard may nevertheless be reached, and take such hold upon legislative and popular acceptance as will insure the same result without infringing the independence of each successive legislature. That such a result, of national purpose, can be reached is shown by the general popular acceptance of the Monroe Doctrine as a national policy. The Monroe Doctrine in itself is a formulated principle; its successive developments have been applications of the principle. So with the navy. The legislature, being representative, would reflect naturally the general purpose of the people as to the standard of naval strength. This would be a national policy, and would appropriate annually in conformity with that policy as conditions continue or change. But that this result of a national naval policy may be attained, an instructed public opinion must be created. This can be done only by insisting upon the international significance of the navy, that being a broad truth which the public can appreciate much more clearly and easily than it can master technical details. As German and French writers have aptly said, navies and armies should be national in the sense that their constitution and numbers reflect a national policy.

Germany has reached such a result. The chain of reasoning which has led to the precise figures is not known; but the first link, the principle, and the last, the application, are known. They affirm essentially that the determination of the aggregate strength of the navy is not merely, nor chiefly, a naval professional attribute; much less a technical one. The decision belongs specifically and above all to those upon whom rests the responsibility of sustaining the international policies of the country. It therefore cannot be governed by naval considerations only, nor by naval men; nor yet solely by the civil committees which in the national legislature represent naval considerations and control naval affairs, narrowly so called. Military and naval provision, to be correct, must reflect the international necessities of the country. Therefore there must enter into these provisions the voices of those who do, or should, make it their business to understand the feelings of other nations and the temper of their governments, which are the essential facts of international relations. With these are to be correlated the feelings of the people of the United States on specific subjects of international friction or ambitions.

The duties of legislation entail as a necessity the subdivision of the whole under special committees. But specialization has its dangers as well as its advantages; and there will exist always two complementary tendencies—that of the special committee to regard its subject as open to no intrusion, to be its business alone, and that of outside members to concede this claim and shove the matter out of their minds with the impression that the responsibility is off their shoulders—which is a mistake. The mistake, however, is so facile and so injurious that some provision is necessary to insure co-operation between committees whose subjects are related; and also between the committees themselves and the executive officers who are concerned with the same subject or subjects.

From what has been said it should be clear that Foreign affairs and Naval affairs have a close interconnection, as well as that each has its own particular sphere of action which does not directly concern the other. All technical considerations, such as tonnage, armament, speed, as well as professional considerations touching the personnel, are in a somewhat narrow sense the attribute of the two Committees on Naval Affairs, as committees. This condition does not exclude in any way the right and duty of any individual member of Congress to attempt to influence these upon the floor of the Houses, but it does indicate a line of severance between the functions of the naval and other committees. But questions of the aggregate power of the navy, and the consequent necessary ratio of annual increase; of the "life" of the heavier ships—that is, their period of useful existence, which evidently bears upon the power of the fleet; of the constitution of the fleet amid several classes of vessels—armored ships, cruisers, torpedo-vessels, and so forth—all these bear upon the power of the nation to hold its course of policy amid the complications of international relations, as well as to insure the protection of its own home coasts and of its transmarine responsibilities. They therefore imply a knowledge not merely of the actual naval force of other states, but of the temper and ambitions of their people and rulers, which ought to be the study not of the Department of State only, but of the committees on Foreign Affairs. I apprehend that nowhere does the separation between the co-ordinate branches of our government operate more disastrously than in the sphere of foreign relations; for this is the subject from which the average Congressman most easily releases his conscience, because it is of the least interest to his constituents and its importance has not come home to his own consciousness.

Mutual intrusion of the several committees upon one another's deliberations would waste time and not tend to harmony. What is needed to meet the exigency is a formal provision by which they shall come together, either as bodies or by representative members, for consultation and interchange of views; that the conclusions of the naval committees upon data peculiar to their own special information and procedure should be duly affected by other data not similarly at their disposal. The naval policy of the country as regards the power of the fleet will not be properly ordered until an arrangement is made by which the foreign relations and naval factors are co-ordinated in some procedure in which both are considered; not only separately, but in connection one with the other. Why one annual battle-ship? or why two? is not a naval question chiefly, if at all. It is a political question, in the sphere of foreign relations. For similar reasons it is necessary that in such procedure the executive and the legislative branches both be represented; for while co-ordinate, and perhaps even because co-ordinate, it is true, as before pointed out, that each represents views contrasted and, in measure, even opposing. Mutual discussion, face to face, is the best remedy for such ills, the best provision to elicit a solution in which the several factors are properly adjusted into a whole, corresponding as nearly as may be to the nation's requirements.

A very striking recognition of the advantage of the

course here advocated is to be found in the recent Imperial Conference between Great Britain and her four self-governing dependencies—Australia, Canada, New Zealand, and South Africa—in May and June, 1911. While many matters of common interest were proposed and discussed, it is known that a dominating consideration in this, as in its predecessors, was that of imperial defense, and the best means of effecting this by a fixed co-operation established between the five communities affected. By general admission, the most significant feature of the procedure was the communication of the actual state of foreign relations, and of their bearing upon the policy of the empire, to the representatives of the several dominions by the British Secretary for Foreign Affairs. In fact, for this occasion the oversea members of the conference sat conjointly in secret session with the British Committee on Imperial Defense, of which the Secretary for Foreign Affairs is a principal member. The connection between foreign relations and the general question of imperial defense by navy and army could scarcely be more signally illustrated, and this view is confirmed by the expressed appreciation of several of the colonial representatives.

It seems so obvious that the military and the naval development of the nation are in some measure co-ordinate that I have thought it inexpedient to devote any of my space to the elaboration of the mutual dependence of army and navy, or the correlation of their functions and strength; the more so that these appear to me less important, and at the same time more obviously apparent to ordinary impression, than the relation existing between naval affairs and diplomacy, in the broad sense which covers all foreign relations. To countries situated as are the United States and Great Britain the element of force in international relations is represented primarily by their navies, though the armies also have their share. It has been well said that the great strength of Great Britain in the Seven Years' War, which determined the future of North America and of India as they are to-day, was that the three co-ordinate factors, army, diplomacy, and navy, were in the hands of one man—the first Pitt. The same was true in reduced measure of Frederick and Napoleon, though neither wielded a competent navy; a fact which was their weakness.

In the long run, however, for purposes of deliberation one man is never equal to several men. We note easily the force of a one-man power; but when he is great and distinguished, in the blaze of his efficiency we realize less easily, though we perfectly well know, the ultimate weakness of unconditioned authority. A dictator may be well enough for six months; for perpetuity and ordinary occasions let us have equals. My old instructor in navigation used to say that the average of a dozen observations is safer than to trust one you think particularly excellent. This is the theory of popular and of representative government in a nutshell. The average judgment of all the people is in the long run better than the judgment of the one wisest. But when deliberation is followed by execution the responsibility of action should be individual.

What is needed, therefore, is not an autocrat, even though he hold power at the will of the people, but a body in which the Army, Foreign Relations, and the Navy are adequately represented; and at the same time the co-ordinate yet opposed functions of government—the executive and the legislature. In Great Britain this result was reached some dozen years ago by the institution of a committee of the cabinet called the Defense Committee. It is presided over by the head of the government, the Prime Minister, and includes always those members of the cabinet to whom in our system correspond the Secretary of State, the Secretary of War, the Secretary of the Navy, and the Secretary of the Treasury. Other members are the Secretaries for the Colonies and for India. To these civil representatives are added four military, two army, and two navy. Like the others, these two are *ex officio;* being the chief among those concerned with the organization, direction, and efficiency of the two military services.

Foreign and colonial interests, which combined constitute the imperial interests of the state, are thus united under one consultative body; and to this civil membership is added adequate representation of the military services. The total, eleven, is more compact than would be possible to us, because each of the civilian members is necessarily in the legislature, as well as charged with executive functions. There therefore is no need to make special provision for representation of the legislature, as there would be if a like scheme were adopted in the United States; for, as has been said, in such a body it is necessary to combine not only civil and military, but executive and legislature in one matured, harmonious decision.

The advisability of adopting such a measure does not rest upon the example of the one other great democratic country besides our own, but upon considerations such as those imperfectly developed in the body of this article. Nevertheless, the need of which the British Defense Committee is the exponent is as real here as there, and it has been satisfied there in large measure by the Defense Committee.

A bill is now before Congress constituting a similar body to be styled a Council of National Defense, with a membership of fourteen. In general principle the proposed constitution of this body represents the same elements as the British—executive, legislature, army, and navy. The most marked difference is that the Secretary of State does not appear in the American scheme. This to me appears regrettable, as not duly recognizing the fundamental consideration of the close connection between Foreign relations and Military development. We also have no functionary equivalent to the British Prime Minister. The British Chief Executive is first among equals, has colleagues; the American President has none. Yet as constitutional Commander-in-Chief of the army and navy he probably has an indefeasible right to take the headship of any such body, while also in himself he sums up all the cabinet attributes, including diplomacy, army, and navy. Should he take the chair in the meetings, all demands would be represented in his one person, while all necessary detailed information would be represented, *ex officio*, by the combination of members. What better provision could be made for counsel to be followed by action?

IV

THE DEFICIENCIES OF LAW AS AN INSTRUMENT OF INTERNATIONAL ADJUSTMENTS

In the previous articles I have endeavored to sustain the thesis that Arbitration, which from its nature and the very etymology of the word presupposes necessarily a tribunal and a code, is not adequate to all the work of Diplomacy, for the final conclusions of which it is proposed as a substitute. I decline entirely to admit that the real opposition is between armaments and arbitration. This is the form of the contention—"law in place of war"— which is attempted to be imposed by those who favor arbitration, not only general but unlimited, on the ground that, as they conceive, all disputes between nations can be brought under the category of legal, by being ranged and classified under a system of laws. My insistence is that this is not possible, because under any classification there cannot but remain always cases in which the right is one of morals and expediency—in other words, of policy —not susceptible of legal definitions, because the preciseness of these deprive them of the elasticity necessary to successful international adjustments; which elasticity diplomacy possesses.

A concrete case, an illustration, is always more easily understood than a general principle. For the purpose of illustration let us take at once the Monroe Doctrine; and in doing so the remark is immediately pertinent that a Monroe Doctrine is by no means the peculiar possession of the United States. During the recent dispute between France and Germany concerning Morocco, a rumor gained currency that France was contemplating the cession to Germany of the Pacific island Tahiti, in part compensation for the relinquishment by Germany of claims to interfere with French action in Morocco. The rumor was probably without foundation, but it aroused immediate jealousy in New Zealand on the ground of local interests. In the New Zealand Parliament a question on the subject was asked by the leader of the opposition. A New Zealand paper said:

The proposal shifts the storm center to our very doors. The planting of another strong German colony in the Pacific, with the added advantage of a suitable naval rendezvous, is fraught with grave issues for New Zealand, for Australia, and even for South America and the United States.

Another journal, not of New Zealand, but of Australia, referring to the rumor,

condemns British apathy in the Pacific in the past, and urges that the Commissioner for Australia, resident in London, be instructed to protest to the imperial government against such a cession.

I guard myself from implying any share in the apprehension concerning the effect upon the United States of a transfer of Tahiti to Germany. When the Caroline and Ladrone Islands were about to be ceded to Germany by Spain, after our war with Spain in 1898, I received more than one letter urging me to use any influence I could exert to induce our government to resist the step. My reply was that, besides having no influence, I saw no sufficient reason for our opposition. But, waiving this personal explanation, in what matter of principle does the objection of New Zealand and of Australia differ from the assured objection of the United States to the acquisition by Germany from Denmark of an island in the West Indies? The reason is the same— namely, the wish to avoid "a storm center at our very doors." But upon what basis of legal right can this be founded? Upon none. How shall a law be imposed making such a sale not legal? The London *Times*, commenting on the New Zealand proposition, said: "Insufficient regard seems to have been paid to the fact that French property, whether in the Pacific islands or elsewhere, is at the sole disposal of France." That is, as regards legal right, Great Britain had no ground for interference. This is substantially what I have said in my second article of this series. Translated into terms of our Monroe Doctrine, the *Times* comment would read, "Insufficient regard seems to be paid to the fact that Danish property, whether in the

West India Islands or elsewhere, is at the sole disposal of Denmark." There is no legal ground for objection, and a tribunal could decide only that the transfer would be lawful and valid. The maintenance of policies such as the Monroe Doctrine must rest upon diplomacy, and its instrument, armament; not upon law. Such special cases afford no reason for changing the general law of nations, which permits the transfer of national territories under many forms.

The British Prime Minister had indicated already in the British Parliament the qualification which policy imposes upon assent to a legal transaction. Any bargain between France and Germany was beyond the scope of British interference, whether by word or deed, unless it should lead to arrangements prejudicial to British interests. In such event, he said, intervention might become "our duty in defense of British interests directly affected by further developments." In other words, the legal right of one country, or of two countries, may so far contravene the natural—that is, the moral—right, the essential interests, the imperative policy, of a third, that resistance would be necessary, and therefore justifiable. Diplomacy then enters, and armament is simply an incident of diplomacy; just as, in an arrangement between two contestants in private life, the fighting power of each, the relative positions of advantage as concerning the matter in dispute, affects the process of the discussion and the ultimate arrangement.

Another curious illustration concerning the Mediterranean has been voiced in ·Austria by an extremist; who, however, has been elected recently president of the Austrian Chamber, as representative of the strongest parliamentary group, and who consequently is a man with a following.

> We Austrian Germans wish to bring about harmony between the Mediterranean Powers. I am coining, perhaps for the first time, an idea. . . . That idea is, the Mediterranean for the Mediterranean Powers. This is directed especially against a Power which has its hands in all the affairs of the world and wants to drive back Germanic Germany.[1]

This is merely individual, without backing in official expression; but, taken in connection with the very large proposed increase in the Austrian navy, officially adopted, and officially designated for Mediterranean service only, the utterance is not without significance; just as Jefferson's early utterance, in some sense comical, seeing his unwillingness to develop force—to back diplomacy with armament— "We begin to broach the idea that all within the Gulf Stream is neutral (*i. e.*, American) waters" was a kind of precursor of the Monroe Doctrine —America for the Americans.

The point I wish to make, however, is that the Monroe Doctrine is a moral question, based upon considerations substantially just, one of natural right, of policy, not of legal right; that a legal standing for it cannot be established by a general code

---

[1] *The Mail,* August 4, 1911, p. 3.

of law, though it may by specific treaty agreements; and that in these respects it does not stand alone, but is reproduced where similar conditions obtain, though not necessarily with equal imperativeness. It is the reflex, as against distant outsiders, of the instinctive impulse toward self-preservation, and as such represents natural right—which is moral right—as opposed to legal. In international affairs this is home rule *versus* centralization, the latter of which is the goal of unlimited arbitration.

If we are to think accurately concerning the sphere of Arbitration, as propounded by its extreme and most logical advocates, we must recognize that the object of their attack necessarily is not armament, but diplomacy. The attempt is to carry all cases into court instead of arranging them outside by compromise or adjustment. It is true that as the case stands the proposition is diplomacy first, arbitration only in case of diplomacy failing; but diplomacy will fail more readily when one of the parties thinks that it will gain substantially by insisting on arbitration—going into court. For instance: if Germany desired to obtain a West India island by purchase from some present owner, and the United States should object, it would be a decided advantage to Germany to transfer the matter from usual diplomatic procedure to a court, controlled in its action by the principles of international law. Consequently, a treaty of general arbitration which enabled her so to do, in case of diplomatic failure to agree, would undoubtedly incline her to persist in disagreement; whereas if the alternative were not a court, but war, many concurrent considerations enter and might incline to agreement. Between individuals, compromises or adjustments are the equivalents of diplomatic negotiation, and proceed, necessarily, partly on grounds of right, partly on grounds of expediency, which recognizes the presence of power—otherwise of force. Each party possesses certain elements of claim, either rightful or plausible, can give a certain amount of trouble, or exercise a certain pressure, or propose a certain equivalent. It is a case of attack and defense quite as really as a military operation, from which it differs exactly as diplomacy, when successful in its normal processes, differs from war. That is, the force is there, is recognized, and is operative. If collision—law-suit—can be avoided, so much the better; but the force has counted all the same.

I refrain, of course, from quoting again the instances cited in previous articles in which diplomacy within recent years has effected adjustments, without war, through silent force; which force has been simply the expression of national power and advantage, used in the instances cited, of Austria and Bulgaria, for ends morally right, but not sustainable in law. National power is surely a legitimate factor in international settlements; for it is the outcome of national efficiency, and efficiency is entitled to assert its fair position and chance of exercise in world matters. It should not be restricted unduly by mere legal tenures dependent for their existing legality upon a prior occupancy; which occupancy often represents an efficiency once existent but long since passed away. The colonial empire of Spain, unimpaired a bare century ago, now wholly disappeared, is a familiar instance. The empire of the Turks is another. The present intervention of Italy in Tripoli is but a further step in a process of which Bosnia, Herzegovina, Bulgaria, are merely the most recent examples. The supplanting of preceding dynasties in India by Great Britain, and her supervision over administration in Egypt, are again illustrations. By what system of law is provision to be made for solving such questions?

Can that which has just been said be condemned fairly as simply a less bald way of affirming that might makes right? No; although certainly it does affirm that the existence of might is no mere casual attribute, but the indication of qualities which should, as they assuredly will, make their way to the front and to the top in the relations of states. Once Prussia counted for less than Holland in international balances. Such qualities, capabilities, not only confer rights, but entail duties, none the less real because not reducible to legal definition; such as the interference of the United States and of Great Britain in 1823 on behalf of South American independence, and of the United States alone, backed by the silent arms of Great Britain, in Cuba in 1898. The competition of such national efficiencies makes for the soundness and equity of the whole international community. It is only when the might of some one state, or ruler, the symbol of its efficiency, becomes unconditioned by opposition, through the exhaustion or recreancy of other nations, that the national efficiency, not meeting competition, tends to abuse and decay like all uncontrolled power. Rome and Carthage, Louis XIV., Napoleon, are familiar instances. Great Britain after Trafalgar illustrated the same uncontrolled power on the seas; but she was saved from decay by the necessity of meeting the opposing forces of the Continent. The Monroe Doctrine itself is such an instance of national force opposing the intrusion of other force in settlements such as have been cited. It is local power asserting that it will withstand the beginnings; will not permit distant power, perhaps mightier than itself, to be established at its very doors in a position involving national danger. This also illustrates the safeguard against the consequences which might be inferred from the proposition that national power, being essentially national efficiency, is entitled to claim its sphere of extension and of opportunity. The co-ordination and balance of international factors—of which the Balance of Power in Europe is the familiar example—like the balances of powers in a Constitution, secure a firmer basis of general welfare than mere legal adjudication, which can be only partially applicable to the community of nations.

It is perhaps a sense of this bearing of the Monroe Doctrine that, in the public discussions of the treaties of general arbitration with Great Britain and France, while pending, caused the doctrine to be characterized as a matter of "domestic policy." I presume the expression must have proceeded from some fairly representative American quarter, as I find it in the Washington correspondence of the London *Times*,[1] the excellence of whose foreign correspondence is known. The correspondent scarcely evolved it from his own inner consciousness. To describe the action of the United States in forbidding one European state to purchase from another European state a piece of its American property—say a West India naval station—as a measure of "domestic" policy has a slightly humorous aspect; and indeed is so characterized by another English paper. Yet in a sense the definition is accurate, because such transfer does affect vital interests as by us conceived, and these may be described inferentially as a matter of domestic policy. Although a case under the Monroe Doctrine is susceptible of legal adjudication by what may be styled the common law of international usage, in no American quarter is there any proposition to submit it to arbitral decision, or even to throw it open to discussion as to its legality; for, as affirmed in its earliest

[1] August 4, 1911.

formulation, it is essential to a sound American policy by a necessity which neither knows nor admits external law.

Curiously and interestingly, simultaneous with the framing of the treaties of general arbitration, in the brief interval between their final conclusion and the signature in Washington, the British government, dealing with the current dispute between France and Germany about Morocco, found itself compelled to a most deliberate and formal pronouncement of its purpose, in all events, to protect "vital interests and national honor," by force if necessary, although the case might present no legal ground for such contingent action.

The representative of the government selected to make this important announcement was the Chancellor of the Exchequer, Mr. Lloyd-George, who cannot be suspected of militarism or of extravagant imperialism. Although a principal member of the same Cabinet, the difference of view in such matters between himself and the Premier, Mr. Asquith, and the Foreign Secretary, Sir Edward Grey, is sufficiently known. It is difficult to believe that there was not deliberate purpose in choosing for the mouthpiece of the government a person so identified with opposition to war, and with expenditures upon social reform which a war would postpone indefinitely. The significance of the occasion was enhanced by the ready extempore speaker reading the carefully worded sentences of his speech.

After expressing, incidentally, his satisfaction at the prospect of a happy issue to the negotiations for a treaty of general arbitration with the United States, Mr. Lloyd-George continued:

But I am also bound to say this—that I believe it is essential in the highest interests, not merely of this country, but of the world, that Britain should at all hazards maintain her place *and her prestige* amongst the Great Powers of the World. Her potent influence has many a time been in the past, and may yet be in the future, invaluable to the cause of human liberty. It has more than once in the past redeemed Continental nations, who are sometimes too apt to forget that service, from over-whelming disaster and even from national extinction. I would make great sacrifices to preserve peace. I conceive that nothing would justify a disturbance of international good-will except questions of the gravest national moment. But if a situation should be forced upon us in which peace could only be preserved by the *surrender of* the great and beneficent *position* Britain has won by centuries of heroism and achievement, by allowing Britain to be treated where her *interests are vitally affected* as if she were of no account in the Cabinet of nations, then I say emphatically that peace at that price would be a humiliation intolerable for a great country like ours to endure. *National honor* is no party question.[1]

The phrases "vital interests" and "national honor," carefully excluded from the recent treaties of general arbitration—the exclusion of which was indeed a chief object of the treaties—appear here again in terms and in full force; not by mere implication, but in distinct assertion relatively to a pending political situation unsettled at the moment of speaking. Nor this alone. Equal stress is laid

[1] *The Mail*, July 24, 1911. My italics.

upon the right of the nation to play its part in the world, to assert itself as a factor in international relations; to sustain by force, by national efficiency, its "position," its "prestige," and its influence among States; to assert the qualities which entitle it to a place in the front; all which are attributes distinct from, and in excess of, such simply inherent rights as vital interests and national honor. No inefficient state could take the same position. The incident is the more significant in that, so far as the public knows, the initiation of the treaties with the United States was due to a member of the same government, Sir Edward Grey, speaking upon the naval ship-building competition between Great Britain and Germany in March, 1911; taking up then and indorsing President Taft's suggestion in the previous December that *all* questions, including vital interests and national honor, should be submitted to judicial arbitration, where such was applicable. Sir Edward Grey's utterance then, being in Parliament, was of course the utterance of the cabinet. That of Mr. Lloyd-George, though not in Parliament, was made under conditions equally responsible.

It appears then that though the phrase "vital interests" may be abandoned, the idea is retained; and not the idea only, but the claim to enforce it beyond all power of interference by any arbitral tribunal. This seems somewhat to illustrate the quaint French proverb, "The more it changes, the more it is the same thing."

Whether named or not, vital interests remain. That is a quality necessarily inherent in vitality; and a nation may refuse to arbitrate them even if it abandons the phrase in a treaty. In our latest treaty with Japan the previous exclusion of Japanese labor immigration was abandoned in terms, but it was well understood that it was to continue in effect; otherwise the treaty could not have been negotiated. Against an immigration distasteful to a large section of its territory the country is now guarded by no legal pronouncement, to which an appeal could be made in court, but simply by an adjustment which neither refers to nor depends upon promulgated law; because such law—which the previous obnoxious treaty represented—would quicken international irritation which simple silence allows to remain dormant. The adjustment is one of diplomacy, which law by interference would merely dislocate.

In view of the various incidents cited here and before, it is apparent that while vital interests and national honor may be submitted at times to judicial arbitration, the field for such submission is greatly limited by specific conditions not amenable to classification. This is the more so, because there are questions, probably many, which, while susceptible of judicial decision because applicable law exists, nevertheless contain chances so contrary to the public interest, to domestic policy, to natural right, one's own or another's—as Cuba in 1898—that reservation of them must be made. Such cases are more easily adjusted by the flexibility of diplomacy than by the rigidity of law.

The solid basis upon which general arbitration may produce beneficial results was well expressed in another speech of Sir Edward Grey's.[1] In this, without formal definition, he indicates the limits which Great Britain feels that expediency places upon treaties having this object in view.

Anything like war between the United States and the British Empire would be so violently opposed to the deepest sentiments and feelings of the people in both countries as to be unthinkable. This made the ground between the two nations especially favorable for an arbitration treaty of an extended kind. If they wished to build a house which was to be secure, he imagined that they would choose to build it on a site which was not liable to earthquakes. There were political as well as territorial earthquakes, but the *respective national policies* of the two countries made it *certain* that they were not liable to political earthquakes; *that there was no conflict of national policy.* In the United States they had no intention of disturbing existing British possessions. They had a policy associated with the name of Monroe, the cardinal point of which was that no European or non-American nation should acquire fresh territory on the continent[2] of America. If it be, as I think it must be, *a postulate of any successful arbitration treaty* of an extended kind that there should be no conflict or possibility of conflict between the national policies of the nations which are parties to it, this condition is assured between us.

In like spirit the London *Spectator* [3] comments:

The United States is the one country in the world our dif-

---

[1] *The Mail,* May 24, 1911. My italics.

[2] It is perhaps well to interpose that the American objection goes beyond the continent, and includes islands geographically American.   [3] August 19, 1911.

ferences with which we can commit to arbitration without any reserve or misgiving, because she is the only country besides our own which is content with the *status quo*.

Most Americans will gladly accept this hopeful prognostic concerning the future relations of the two nations; yet Sir Edward Grey's speech by its reservations sufficiently shows that in his judgment the General Arbitration Treaty between Great Britain and the United States cannot safely be accepted in Great Britain as a type for all occasions and all nations. As to Great Britain herself, it may be well to remember a recent very distinct divergence of political view, in which the Senate of the United States prevented the nation from committing itself to a treaty which might have proved extremely awkward at the present moment.

In 1900 the Executive of the day concluded the Hay-Pauncefote Treaty, by which the long-standing Clayton-Bulwer Treaty was modified and the particular interest of the United States in the Panama Isthmus and Canal recognized. The Senate, in ratifying, did not insist upon the right to fortify; but it introduced three changes in the treaty, one of which provided that nothing in the text should be construed to "apply to measures which the United States may find it necessary to take for securing by its own forces the defense of the United States and the maintenance of public order." That is, the proviso reserved the right to defend, but not the right to prepare for defense by erecting fortifications. Great Britain refusing to accept the changes, negotiation was resumed, and in the second draft the clause forbidding fortification was omitted; Great Britain thus assenting by silence to their erection, and, as the diplomatic correspondence shows, with full understanding that she thus did concede the right to fortify. This is the treaty which now fixes the relations of the two countries with reference to the Panama Canal.

If the first treaty had been accepted as it stood when signed, the United States would have been bound by it as part of the law of the land; and as part of the law of nations so far as the relations of the United States and Great Britain are concerned. The Executive of 1900 was willing then to abandon a claim upon which the Executive of 1911 strongly desired to act, and is acting, with the support of Congress. The Senate of 1900 saved the situation for 1911. A treaty is for the period of its duration a law; and the two situations, prior and subsequent to the acquisition of the Canal Zone, show the deficiencies of law as an instrument in international adjustments through its unsuitableness to a future and changed condition. The lesson, indeed, is not that treaties should never be made, but that they should be entered upon cautiously, and should contain reasonable provision of time expiry, so as not indefinitely to fetter national action. Although the site of the proposed fortification has now become

United States territory, which in 1900 it was not, the first treaty, if ratified, would have afforded at least a basis for opposition by Great Britain to the legality of fortification; and there is also no certainty that her silence on the matter even under the second treaty proves consent, as a legal proposition, then or now. Subsequent cession does not relieve territory from previous liens upon it of a third party, just as the sale of a house does not invalidate a pre-existing mortgage. Even under all existing conditions the right to fortify has been disputed by eminent authority in the United States. If a treaty of general arbitration had been in force when the decision to fortify was reached, what—under the first treaty at least—would there have been to prevent Great Britain demanding arbitration, and insisting that in its judgment the question was open to legal adjudication because of the treaty; although since its ratification the Canal Zone, the site of the fortifications, has become United States territory? Only the postulate stated by Sir Edward Grey—the absence "of conflict between the national policies."

Referring to general arbitration, the Chancellor of the German Empire, whose position corresponds to that of the Prime Minister of Great Britain, as nearly as the very different political constitutions of the two countries admit, said in the Reichstag:[1]

As regards the clause about honor and vital interests, I am convinced that the abolition of the clause does not create peace,

[1] *The Mail*, March 31, 1911.

but merely constitutes an assertion that a serious occasion for a breach of the peace between the two nations concerned *is unthinkable. An unlimited arbitration treaty merely puts the seal upon a state of things already existing de facto.* Let this state of things change, let there arise between the two nations antagonisms which touch their vital interests, then I would like to see the arbitration treaty that does not burn like tinder. . . . The condition of peaceableness is strength.

These words reproduce essentially the qualifications expressed by Sir Edward Grey two months later, and they are emphasized by the antagonism— the "change in the state of things"—which has grown up between Germany and Great Britain within a generation. From the coincidence of opinions between two statesmen in such eminent position, reinforced by the pronouncements of Mr. Asquith and Mr. Lloyd-George already quoted, which applied directly to a country between which and Great Britain the friendliest relations existed up to less than thirty years ago, there can be inferred not only the transitoriness of international relations, but the insecurity of treaties of general arbitration when situations undergo radical alteration.

Otherwise, the legal bond of treaty, far from ameliorating conditions, would have tended only to exasperation. This was abundantly shown by the increasing irritation in the United States over the Clayton-Bulwer Treaty during the two or three decades preceding its supersession.

Historical illustration, which is simply the citation of cases and precedents, amply proves the insufficiency of law as an instrument in composing differences. By insufficient I do not mean that it is not sufficient in many instances, possibly in a majority; but that the exceptions are so numerous that legal classification cannot fully embrace them, and therefore another instrument than law, than arbitration, is in such cases required. In the matter of instruction, no theoretic discussion, however ample and lucid, affords a substitute for historical illustration.

Several such illustrations of very recent date have been adduced in this and previous articles. One much more ancient, yet entirely analogous, and demonstrative that the instrument used must be adapted to the end in view, is afforded by the history of liberty in England. The early Stuart kings, notably Charles I., with great care based their oppressive actions upon law; upon law obsolete, in the sense that the progress of the nation had rendered inapplicable methods which in previous years had been applicable, but still law existing unrepealed. International law, as law, has similarly to treat as legal a claim which may have issued in intolerable conditions. Claims of such character could have been alleged for the forcible retention of the American colonies by Great Britain, and of the Spanish colonies by Spain, up to and including the deliverance of Cuba; and such law must govern any tribunal. The judge decides what the law is, not what it should be.

Concerning the Stuart oppression, the latest and

most distinguished historian of the period, Dr. Rawson Gardiner, after remarking that "it was impossible to allow any mere interpretation of the law to decide the question at issue" between King and Parliament, uséd an illustration which in the light of the events of the year 1911 is singularly striking.

Suppose it should happen that the House of Lords placed itself in deliberate opposition to the House of Commons, even after a general election had shown that the House of Commons was in accord with the feelings of the constituencies. Suppose that the House of Lords rejected every bill sent up to it by the Commons. What would be the use of applying to the judges as arbitrators? They could but decide that the Lords were legally in the right. They could not decide whether they were politically in the right.

Since Dr. Gardiner wrote, the imagined case has occurred, not in all particulars, but in substance. The inadequacy of the law has been recognized; and the British government of to-day has obtained by political action, of the nature of threatened constitutional violence, the result to which law, as an instrument, proved inadequate. A political instrument was employed when the legal instrument—recourse to a court—could not but fail. In the case of the Stuarts the political instrument used was armed resistance.

The recent result to the House of Lords is a warning to conservative forces everywhere, national and international, to recognize betimes the need of specific changes in law, which shall adapt it to those shiftings in social and other conditions that conflict with and defy particular legal enactments; or to international situations which have become obsolete, or are becoming so. A danger in the path of arbitration, of legal decisions as opposed to diplomatic arrangements, is that existing political differences will be brought to the bar, not merely of laws applicable but outworn, but of legal tenures based on antiquated or obsolete conditions formerly suitable to times and circumstances but which no longer are so. Law lacks elasticity, not merely because of the time needed to pass new legislation, but because it itself, at least in international relations, may be correct as a general proposition, yet cannot always be applied satisfactorily to a particular case. In such instances a different instrument is required. A political *impasse* must be met by a special provision, by measures which shall proceed on a basis not of strict legality, but of evident necessary expediency; in short, by diplomacy rather than by law.

In the intercourse of nations diplomacy is the analogue of the discussions out of Parliament which preceded the recent use of force by one party to this dispute. In the one kind of contention, as in the other, recognized force lay in the background. It is in neither a principal; in both it is an agent. The positiveness inherent in the very idea of law, its lack of elasticity, renders it too frequently inadequate to the settlement of certain classes of disputes, because in them an accepted law exists, decision in accordance with which would simply perpetuate injustice or sustain intolerable conditions.

V

In the preceding articles of this series, the attempt has been to sustain the thesis that the interrelations of independent states are not susceptible of full establishment, nor of all necessary adjustment from time to time, upon a basis of law. This is partly because law, whatever the method of its development, whether by custom or statute, cannot be so systematized beforehand as to cover all cases; partly because unforeseen conditions arising, or gradual changes of conditions evolving, existing law is by them outgrown. Thus law often lags behind conditions, and often overlives them. In either case there results an inapplicability, from which the attempt to decide by law would work actual injustice.

The Monroe Doctrine, frequently cited because peculiarly American, illustrates both phases. During our colonial era, and for thirty years after the adoption of the constitution, European powers colonized, conquered, exchanged territories in the American hemisphere, without eliciting from the United States serious opposition based upon a recognized principle. Throughout the period named the conditions which gave origin to the doctrine were unforeseen. These conditions were the revolt of the Spanish-American colonies, involving a future independence of a large part of the American continents, and the intention of the so-called Holy Alliance of European continental states to reduce them to their former allegiance by force of arms. In resistance to this attempt Great Britain and the United States acted in common, though not in concert, and with distinct purpose to use force, if needed. The purpose of the Holy Alliance was not in contravention of law as law then was, nor, as far as I know, as law now is; but in more than one point it traversed the policy of the United States and of Great Britain as determined by the changed conditions. That policy was partly one of particular national interest, as understood by each of the protesting nations; partly one of common sympathy with peoples struggling for relief from a very real oppression. There can be little doubt on which side law lay, nor on which justice was. Right was sustained by policy and by a conviction of rightfulness; the instrument of sustainment being diplomacy through its ordinary channels, backed by force.

The unforeseen conditions which diplomacy and force met thus successfully, and to which law as it then stood was inadequate, were followed by gradual changes. These changes were chiefly in the growing population and wealth of the United States, and in the recognition by her people of the expediency of excluding European quarrels from propagation to this hemisphere; on the same principle that a man is disinclined to see a fire spread in the direction of his own house. As remarked by a New Zealand paper quoted in the fourth of these articles, we objected to "storm centers at our doors." Upon this view, at the very moment of pronouncement of the Monroe Doctrine, we based the assertion that the American continents were not in future to be open to further European colonization. This determination to maintain the *status quo* of the moment received gradual extension afterward. The denial of colonization was advanced to the denial of the appropriation of American territory in any manner; by conquest in war, or by sale, or by exchange—a further change of conditions. Each of these processes of transfer is a common international transaction, and perfectly lawful by to-day's accepted standards of international law; witnessed, for instance, by such recent events as our own purchase of the Philippines, the conquest of Algiers by France, her military occupation of Morocco, and, incident to the latter, the exchange of African territories between her and Germany.

In America conditions continued to change. At the first Great Britain had rejected the pronouncement against colonization. Hence the coincident action of the two governments against the European alliance had been merely one of momentary expediency, based on divergent motives. British opposition to the spirit of the Monroe Doctrine continued, and was protracted throughout the duration of intestinal strife over slavery. This weakened the vigor which otherwise might have been shown by the United States, in virtue of her steady increase in power and of her favorable geographical position. Of this instability of policy the Clayton-Bulwer Treaty of 1850 was in its day the exponent. Not till the national unity had been consolidated, by the results of the War of Secession, was the diplomatic contest with Great Britain maintained with a resolution which issued in the formal supersession of the Clayton-Bulwer Treaty by that of 1901, known as the Hay-Pauncefote.

Doubtless changing conditions in Europe as well as in America, and changing phases of national sentiment, inclining the English-speaking peoples more toward co-operation and less toward opposition, had their part in the general result, favoring the long-established policy of the United States which has been considered. The course of events has been thus summarily outlined, not to revive old antagonisms, but to illustrate that the happy issue has been reached by diplomacy, which deals in arrangements, not by law, which dictates by decisions; and that law throughout was incompetent to deal with situations as they changed. This has been so because there was no law, nor at present does there exist any law, to which the United States could have appealed in support of a position she was determined to maintain. All precedent, all the general custom of nations, has been and is against a course which undoubtedly has contributed to the quietness of the Western World; because it has settled that it is useless for either of two European belligerents to seize an American dependency of the other, unless prepared to encounter also the armed resistance of the United States.

In this particular, the law of nations had outlived the conditions of colonial America and those of the first forty years of national existence of the United States. Conditions had changed, and law had not kept pace with them. Only by specific treaty, accepting the doctrine as binding on both parties, could it be given a statutory position recognizable as determinative by an arbitral court. But no such treaty has been made, nor at the critical moments could have been negotiated. Whether a long-continued acquiescence, or at least absence of contestation, and if so, how long, could be construed by such a court to constitute an established custom equivalent to a law, I am unable to say; and I fancy the court itself would be puzzled to decide, in view of the correspondence on the Venezuela boundary in 1895. Even if such a point has been reached now, which is more than doubtful, it certainly had not during by far the greater part of the period of dispute. The final adjustments have been by diplomacy, unaided by law, yet influenced by force.

FORCE IN INTERNATIONAL RELATIONS

The Monroe Doctrine is a policy, not a law, and
behind it has always lain force, not the less real
because not flaunted.   The most characteristic illustration of this was in 1866, when the hundreds of
thousands who had fought the War of Secession were
still in the prime of their vigor and experience.
Then the United States compelled Napoleon III.
to evacuate Mexico, but without moving a soldier or
expressing a menace.   Indeed, force is never more
operative than when it is known to exist but is not
brandished.   Of this General Schofield's mission in
1865–66 afforded an interesting illustration.   The
object was "to see if the French Emperor could not
be made to understand the necessity of withdraw-
ing his army from Mexico, and thus save us the
necessity of expelling it by force."[1]   The intimation
was conveyed, and the result obtained; but in a manner so void of offense that the ultimate agent, force,
can scarcely be said to have appeared.   It is often
asserted that the existence of the armed forces of
Europe, one over against the other, is provocative
of war.   They might be, they probably would be,
if during negotiation or in a moment of excitement
they were paraded in threatening manner.   Sensible
men, however, know well that other sensible men
will avoid a known danger, unless circumstances
are such that avoidance may be taken to show a
yielding to fear; and therefore, unless desirous of
collision for specific reasons, as Bismarck was in

[1] Schofield's *Forty-Six Years in the Army,* p. 382.

1870, they prefer to carry their point by discussion, in which the factor of force is ignored yet understood.

Can then force, broadly considered, be regarded as an inevitable factor in international adjustments and in the maintenance of the general international balances? The point is interesting, especially at this present moment when the apparent inclination of public sentiment throughout that which we esteem the civilized world, the world of the highest development in material progress and in artistic and literary culture, is tending toward the elimination of that active display of force which we call war. May it not be that in confounding force with war we are simply ignoring a fact of not only general but universal existence? Law itself, which its extreme advocates desire to see installed in place of war, is, in last analysis, simply force regulated—a most desirable end—but inadequate for the very reason that it is only one manifestation of a power which is manifold in its exhibition. Not only does law for its efficacy depend upon force, as is shown by the entire paraphernalia of justice from the single policeman to the final court of appeal, but under law and within law force continually controls.

In this country we have recently been passing through, and have not yet emerged from, a period in which force, astutely managed and directed, has largely controlled the business relations of the entire community. The force of concentrated capital

is as real and as material as the force of an organized
army, and it has the same advantage over a multi-
tude of unorganized competitors that an army has
over a mob. At times well within memory the contest has narrowed down to a conflict almost personal, at times quite personal, between concentrated
financial powers, ending at times in a disabling
reverse or disastrous overthrow to one or the other.
As the disadvantage of such contests has become
apparent to the greater competitors, there has succeeded a disposition to co-operation, corresponding
to alliance between political entities for their mutual
benefit. Coalescence of force dominates more and
more, until the mass of individuals constituting the
community realize that such force menaces their
independence and must be opposed by other force;
the force of money by the force of votes expressing
itself in legislation. This is the condition to-day—
the condition of regulation. Yet it is realized that
for the benefit of the whole the force of concentrated
capital must be permitted free play within certain
limits, which are fixed by the opposing forces of the
ballot-box.

The states of the world of European civilization,
in which America is included, in their organized
national activities represent among themselves an
international community of competing business organizations. They recognize that the general benefit depends ultimately upon the welfare of each
and all; but nevertheless the aim of each is to com-

pass for itself—that is, for its people—the utmost preponderance of advantage possible to be secured. Of this aim and effort, Protection, technically so called, is the most evident and the crudest manifestation. Protection is simply the use of force, of national power recognized as legal, to secure commercial advantage; but it becomes immediately apparent that, so far as the system is economically sound, the greater the area that can be embraced within it—that is, the larger the concentration—the more effective is the operation.

Hence results inevitably the attempt to enlarge the national boundaries, in order to include and to administer to the national advantage as much territory at least as can be securely held and profitably exploited. The motives thereto, though not purely economical, are largely so; but undoubtedly there does co-operate the perfectly human and universal motive of enjoyment in mere possession, and in the activities of administration and exploitation. These must be taken into account as real and influential national factors. It is a mistake to argue that because nations and peoples are largely animated by self-interest, self-interest alone moves them; and it is a blunder to infer that there is inconsistency in maintaining the predominance of interested motive, and at the same time affirming the existence of other and competing impulses. Both classes exist. If there be inconsistency here, as is sometimes asserted, the inconsistency is not in the statement, but in the human nature concerning which the statement is made.

The wars of the past half-century bear witness to this; for it may safely be affirmed that self-interest, especially of the pecuniary order, bore in them a relatively small part. The American War of Secession was with both parties one mainly of sentiment; on the one side the objection to see its country dismembered, on the other the instinct of self-preservation, as misunderstood, and of independence as essential to self-preservation. Bismarck's wars of 1864, 1866, and 1870 were motived, doubtless, by the interest of Germany; but they embraced a conception of German racial unity consolidated into political unity which, while assuredly a utilitarian end, was certainly not devoid of a lofty nobleness to which German sentiment responded with an exaltation that ennobled the wars themselves. The war of Russia against Turkey, in 1877, no doubt took account of Russian ambitions concerning Constantinople; but the determining impulse, which constrained even the autocratic Tsardom, was popular sentiment inflamed by sympathy with the oppression of near-by kindred peoples. A similar impulse dictated the war between Spain and the United States; the transfer of the Philippines, the chief material gain, if so it can be called, not only was not an object of the war, but was accepted with reluctance, under an unwilling sense of duty, as one of its unfortunate results. Various motives, some of them sordid, may have entered into the transactions preceding the war between Great Britain and the Boer republics; but the shuffling, invidious handling of the Uitlander franchise by the Boer government was the predominating factor. The author of *The Great Illusion* shows clearly enough that much is now done in South Africa contrary to the views of the British government, an inevitable result of local self-government, especially where there is a color question; but the constitution of South Africa establishes equality of suffrage, in its basis and in its exercise, among all adult white males. This did not exist in the Transvaal before the war, of which it is one of the great gains. Union and equality are thus the outcome of war. The war between Japan and Russia I believe to have been felt by Japan one of national self-preservation. That sentiment prevailed among her people, and not without reason.

It is, I believe, the cardinal mistake of the author of *The Great Illusion* that nations now go to war, or are preparing for war, under the impression that there is financial profit in injuring a neighbor. His other proposition, that the extension of national territory—that is, the bringing a large amount of property under a single administration—is not to the financial advantage of a nation, appears to me as illusory as to maintain that business on a small capital is as profitable as on a large. It is the great amount of unexploited raw material in territories politically backward, and now imperfectly possessed by the nominal owners, which at the present moment constitutes the temptation and the impulse to war of European states. The difficulty of the situation, from the point of view of the advocate of disarmament, is that law is not competent to the solution, while diplomacy is; and that in diplomacy force is always a factor. The recent difficulty between France and Germany, and its method of solution —in fact, the whole Morocco question during the past ten years—illustrate this series of propositions.

As the motives of the several wars cited rose far above a mere financial advantage, so their results have been beneficial from a nobler point of view. The preservation of the North American Union, with the abolition of the degradation of mankind in slavery, and of the disastrous economical condition of slave labor; the welding of the German race into the German nation, followed by the great industrial and economic advance, which only a unified administration could have insured; the detachment of Bosnia, Herzegovina, and Bulgaria from the rule of Turkey, the benefit to the inhabitants of those provinces, attested by the results and newly witnessed to in recent years by the miseries of Albania under continued Turkish rule; the advantage to Cuba, Porto Rico, and the Philippines from the substitution of American influence, or American control, for that of Spain; the opportunity of Japan, and her national security, purchased by the successes in Manchuria at a money cost far exceeding in pro-

portion that of any of the other wars named—all
these are instances of benefits secured by war, and
which could not have been secured by law, for in
no one of the cases was there a law which could
have accomplished the specific result.

Law could not have abolished slavery; could not
have given the impetus which achieved German
unity; could not have dispossessed Turkey of her
misgoverned territories, nor Spain of hers; could not
have extorted from the Krüger *régime* fair treatment
for the foreigner, nor established equal rights in
South Africa as it was; could not have vindicated the
natural rights of Japan against the encroachments
of Russia in the Far East. Diplomacy using force
accomplished in these instances results to which
law was unequal, and could not but be; while
diplomacy not actually using force, but holding
it always in reserve, is continually effecting adjustments where law cannot pronounce decisions. Treaties, conventions, diplomatic agreements of every
kind, are of the nature of lawmaking, of constituting
for present conditions a formula which shall have the
force of law; but lawmaking is a different thing
from a legal decision. Lawmaking is the function
of diplomacy; legal decision that of arbitration.
The great objection to law, however, is not merely
that it is inadequate, but that in most of the above
cases it would have been inequitable—would have
perpetuated injustice by sanctioning outworn conditions or inapplicable principles.

The extension of national control in order to further national advantage, or to flatter national self-esteem, is a natural outcome of Protection. That the same disposition is observed in the great non-protectionist state—Great Britain—shows how deeply the fundamental idea of Protection is rooted in human nature. But here enters that other universally recognized factor—that forces take the line of least resistance. Probably no state in Europe at the present time seriously contemplates the acquisition by force of the European territory of a rival. In this assumption I do not reckon Turkey as European. Alsace and Lorraine are probably the last examples of such transfer. The reason is plain. Such acquisition cannot be so valuable industrially as to compensate for the expense of the conquest. The armaments of European states now are not so much for protection against conquest as to secure to themselves the utmost possible share of the unexploited or imperfectly exploited regions of the world—the outlying markets, or storehouses of raw material, which under national control shall minister to national emolument. The case is much like that of the ownership of ore-fields by the Steel Trust, of which we have heard so much; the natural, and certainly not unwise, wish of the manufacturer to command his own sources of fuel and raw materials.

But while the scene of such acquisition is elsewhere than in Europe, it is in Europe that the battle is fought. The whole dispute about Morocco is one about colonial empire, as contributory to the advantage of the nations concerned. The solvent is force, because there is no basis of law upon which the question can be settled. As regards the administration of Morocco, the only law applicable is that of the right of the present possessor, which, if capable of maintainment, would simply relegate the territories in dispute to the barbarous anarchy and inutility which has been their lot for centuries past. The redemption to mankind of Algiers, Egypt, India, is the warrant in equity for the forcible suppression of those who previously occupied and controlled, but failed to justify their possession by results. "Cut it down. Why cumbereth it the ground?" Even the author of *The Great Illusion* holds that co-operation in the subjugation of the planet, the utilization of its resources, is the true warfare of man, and, if I rightly understand him, admits that communities which do not contribute to this may be taken in hand gently and administered temporarily to that end.[1] But what decides which among several competitors shall be the administrator? Force simply; not only the military force of organized armies and navies, but force of position, or of previous incidents which have given one or another a certain priority of intervention, or advantage of neighborhood, as of France against Germany in the Morocco imbroglio. In the adjust-

[1] *The Great Illusion*, p. 247.

ments which take place, armed force, and that in distant Europe itself, has the casting vote either to maintain or to reverse; and in Europe, not in the remote dependency, would collision take place.

The " Open Door," a modern phrase, is another outcome of this desire to increase area in order to gain economic advantage. The Open Door is the reply of other parties to the intervener and appropriator, and the open door depends for maintenance upon force. The open door might be defined briefly as the international retort to protection. Equality of opportunity is demanded; but the demand rests upon force—force possessed with the purpose to use it, if necessary.

It is to be noted in this connection that the outward impulse of the European nations results naturally from the internal competitions of Europe itself; from the settled conditions of political ownership, and from the overtaking of resources by population through a diminution of the one and an increase of the other; both of which are the inevitable result of continued peace and industrial advance. The very high development of corporate efficiency characteristic of Christian civilization as a whole, an efficiency partly political, partly industrial, partly, it is probable, composed of some third factor not so easy to name or define, not only requires ampler fields, but is from its own very nature impatient of surrounding inefficiencies, and disposed to disregard such figments as legal right, based upon mere useless prior occupancy, to territory which there is neither the intention nor the political capacity to utilize.

In short, competition for control is extending its sphere from the scene of European civilization to that of extra-European, and exists not only between the European peoples themselves in these exterior regions, but between the present occupants and the intruders. It is there a competition not merely of nations, as in Europe and in America, but of civilizations, and of the religions which have stamped their essential characteristics upon the nations professing them. Of the Christian religion the great constituent is power; which in another shape, easily assumed, becomes force. Force is power in action. We are prone to assume that, because the personal ideal of the individual Christian, exemplified above all in the Master, is abnegation of self, therefore power and force are alien from the Christian scheme of character. The history of the Master Himself refutes this. The distinction between the Christian conception and that of its strongest rival in the outside world—Islam—is that of the entrance of the human will into the Divine accomplishment. The conception of Christianity is not the arbitrary will of the Creator, the kismet of the Mohammedan, but the purpose of the Creator conditioned by man's energy in willing co-operation.

Abnegation of self evidently finds its correlative in social impulse. The one implies the other. Hence the co-operative impulse, the disposition to efficient organization, proceeds logically from the conception of man's part in the regeneration of the world. This tendency to efficient organization is a faculty wholly distinct from the personal qualities of the individual members of certain races which do not show the same capacity for organization; such as the Chinese or the Turks. To right what is amiss, to convert, to improve, to develop, is of the very essence of the Christian ideal. Without man's responsive effort, God Himself is—not powerless—but deprived of the instrument through which alone He wills to work. Hence the recognition that, if force is necessary, force must be used for the benefit of the community, of the commonwealth of the world. This fundamental proposition is not impaired by the fact that force is best exercised through law, when adequate law exists. Except as the expression of right, law is an incubus. Hence much of the present magnification of law is the mere worship of a fetich.

To such a view aggression, in its primary sense of onward movement, is inevitable. Those who will not move must be swept aside. They may be drawn into the movement by moral forces, as Japan has been; but if not, they must be brought despite themselves into external conditions favorable to their welfare and the general good, as has been done in India, in Egypt, and in the Philippines. As toward conviction of the intellect, upon which religion depends, force is inoperative and the use of it therefore wicked. Christianity as a religious system rests, consequently, upon a different power—a spiritual. But to Christianity as a political system, force, the sword if necessary, is incumbent, if required to remedy environment, to amend external conditions; just as the force underlying law is used to ameliorate social evils.

Recent organized attempts to convert the Church of Christ in the United States into a political engine for control of political results, in a reported difference of opinion between the Executive and the Senate, call for some plain speaking as to the attitude of Jesus Christ toward the use of force for the remedy of evils. The question is thought to be decided by the application to Him of the title "Prince of Peace." This is a pure begging of the question. Not only is there much imagery associating Him with actual force, even with war, but the phrase cited occurs but once in the Bible, in a Jewish prophecy which the Church has delighted to apply to Christ; but the context shows that the person to whom the words immediately refer is a deliverer whose justice reposes upon power, and by whom, or for whom, a forcible deliverance has been wrought from the yoke of an oppressor. Moreover, this understanding of the prophecy dominated the thought of the Jews who accepted it. The peace of Jesus Christ, as He distinctly said, is not as the world giveth. It is the inward peace of the individual resting upon God. This He called emphatically "My peace." The sway of this will be co-extensive with any community so far as the individuals thereof seek it; but in the presence of evil the genius of Christianity is aggressive.

The progress of the changes which the impact of Christianity on the world produces will probably be gradual. It has been so in the past, little by little, with a recent accelerated pace; conditioned by the *vis inertiæ* of the exterior peoples, by the active opposition aroused in them, and by the contemporary rivalries within the Christian commonwealth. Two principal influences will characterize the movement, as they have from the beginning: the influence of ideas and the influence of force. In broad generalization, the Christian Church falls within the first category, the Christian state within the second. Missionary effort is the exponent of the one, armament of the other. The two organizations, church and state, and their several offices, are too easily confused in discussion, particularly of the philanthropic order. Their spheres are different; and when the church, as church, interferes with the state, as state, whether in men's thoughts or in their acts, evil follows. The people of the United States scarcely realize what a potent political agency a church may be made; and the Christian Church scarcely realizes the injury it will do itself by diverting any of its none too great activity from spiritual ministration to political agitation.

In the past, in other lands, the church not infrequently has evoked the sword of the state. To-day she seeks to shatter it. In either case she errs. The present discipline of the sword in international relations keeps alive armament and the organization of force—the power of the sword—which alone centuries ago checked and rolled back the Saracenic and Turkish invasions. Upon this depends the ability to use force in the great conflict with the powers of political evil in the external world. In days not long past I have written of this as prospective. To-day it is upon us. In it the disarmament of the states of European civilization, the abandonment of the energies of force, will mean the downfall of that civilization.

VI

"THE GREAT ILLUSION"

In the early months of the year 1911 appeared a book called *The Great Illusion*,[1] which attracted at the time much attention and approval, which it probably still commands.

I have read the book twice attentively. Owing to the number of topics incidentally discussed, I have found difficulty in realizing to myself the precise thread of the argument. The author, however, in two instances at least has defined the purpose of the work in words of his own. I say in words of his own, because he has chosen, not unwisely, to preface his conception of "the great illusion," which he thinks prevails widely, by numerous illustrative quotations from others, whom he constitutes his antagonists in idea. Based upon these citations,

---

[1] It may be said, in explanation of this article, that the book with which it deals, *The Great Illusion*, by Norman Angell, was published in the early months of 1911. My criticism of it appeared in *The North American Review* of March, 1912, and Mr. Angell's "Reply," in the same magazine, in the following June. As the article now stands, it contains additional remarks, which on account of space were omitted from the first publication, together with some comment elicited by Mr. Angell's "Reply."

he then summarizes (p. 29) the illusion which he detects in them as being

one of the universally accepted axioms of European politics—namely, that a nation's financial and industrial stability, its security in commercial activity—in short, its prosperity and well-being—depend upon its being able to defend itself against the aggression of other nations, who will, if they are able, be tempted to commit such aggression because in so doing they will increase *their* power, and consequently *their* prosperity and well-being, at the cost of the weaker and vanquished.[1]

Again (p. 336):

At the root of the whole armament difficulty lies the theory that economic advantage goes with the exercise of military force; in other words, armaments exist as the logical outcome of that illusion with which this book deals.

I believe that the thesis thus defined is erroneous in at least two particulars. First, as a matter of fact, economic advantage frequently has accompanied the use of military force, and resulted from it. Two conspicuous instances of this afforded by history are: the supremacy of Great Britain as a financial and industrial community, due mainly to the predominance of her military sea power during the eighteenth century to the fall of Napoleon in 1815, and the economical development of Germany following upon the war with France in 1870–71. Second, the purpose of armaments in the minds of those maintaining them is not primarily economical advantage, in the sense of depriving a neighboring

[1] Italics here are the author's, not mine.

state of its own, or fear of such consequence to itself through the deliberate aggression of a rival having that particular end in view.   The object is the assertion of right in doubtful questions which are continually arising, largely from the progressive exploitation of unutilized regions of the world.   In illustration, it is necessary only to cite, as very recent or still pending, the questions of Tripoli, Morocco, and China, with the open door.   Between the states of European civilization these are not questions of legal right and wrong; because no law exists, no valid title.   Titles are being made by international agreements, but the agreements themselves, in the process of development and at the moment of making, are conditioned by force.   In connection with these, disputes are continually arising which more than once have led close to war.   It is true that, should war come, the scene would be chiefly in Europe, and that provision against financial and economical dangers thence arising is one principal motive to armament; but it is not true that aggression upon the financial and economical system of another state is the motive for armament anywhere.

The particular point of view of the book, which has led both to the selection of the quotations from opponents (pp. 17–28), and also to the definitions of *The Great Illusion*, just cited in the author's words, is further illustrated by two passages.   Thus (p. 77): "The real basis of social morality is self-interest": that is, as the proverb more tersely puts it, "Honesty is the best policy."

Again (p. 370):

> Is not the root of the profound distrust of, and hostility to, the peace man, that his plea has been made rather on the basis of altruism than of interest, on morality rather than of policy? The man in the street is firmly convinced that he is being asked to surrender some solid interest in favor of morality—sentiment, as he would call it.

It may be said, then, that the main argument of the book proceeds on the basis that the solid bottom fact in international relations is regard to material self-interest, and that "the great illusion" is that material self-interest can be advanced by the use of force—either by fighting, or by the armaments which, by showing force at hand, prevent fighting yet compass desired ends.

These remarks and quotations can be taken to define the general topic of the book. Before proceeding to discuss it, and to comment upon certain particularities, or details of the argument, it may be best to state at once the very different point of view from which the present writer approaches the matter. I hold that the interest of the nation is indeed the business of the government, but that the danger of war proceeds mainly from the temper of the people, which, when roused, disregards self-interest. In every country the government, in that guardianship of the interests of the state which we call policy, pursues a certain line of conduct.

This results in friction with the policy of another country. As discussion proceeds, each government, deeply conscious of the evils of war, endeavors to reach a solution of peace; but to the people the matter gradually assumes the aspect of a right and a wrong, and popular feeling, disregardful of that particular self-interest which peace represents, is wrought up to a pitch of supporting by arms its asserted right —that other self-interest which is commonly defined as self-respect, or honor. The history of the year 1911 illustrates these positions. It has been apparent that the governments of France, Germany, and Great Britain have earnestly striven for peace; that their several stands were taken rather on the ground of national right than of immediate economic advantage; and that the moods of the several peoples answered more readily to the feeling of national honor at stake than to any supposed material self-interest.

[This paragraph met by anticipation the allegation of an inconsistency on my part, made by the author of *The Great Illusion* in the opening pages of his "Reply."[1] The policy of governments, now as always—now as when Washington penned the remark—must be dictated by the interests of the nation. This is an entirely different proposition from that of *The Great Illusion*, that the purpose of armaments to-day is primarily a supposed economical advantage, either by deliberate aggression upon the

[1] *The North American Review*, June, 1912.

possessions of another state or from fear of such aggression on the part of a rival.]

In short, the inciting causes of war in our day are moral; a statement which includes of course immoral, as both adjectives, though opposite in meaning, as are "good" and "bad," belong to the same category of motives. The war of the United States against Spain is held by some Americans to have been unjust, and therefore immoral; by others, among whom myself, to have been illustriously moral; but by neither, I apprehend, can it be seriously maintained to have been inspired by material self-interest. The American government tried earnestly to avoid it, believed that it could be avoided; deceived therein, I think, by failure to appreciate Spanish diplomatic methods as illustrated by history. The people forced the issue. In the fifth article of this series I have cited *seriatim* the principal wars of the last half-century as proceeding demonstrably from motives essentially moral. Even where material self-interest is at the bottom of the trouble, as possibly in the present state of feeling between Germany and Great Britain, it is less the loss endured than the sense of injustice done, or apprehended, that keeps alive the flame.

I believe, therefore, that the fundamental proposition of the book is a mistake. Nations are under no illusion as to the unprofitableness of war in itself; but they recognize that different views of right and wrong in international transactions may provoke

collision, against which the only safeguard is armament. Unarmed, or inadequately armed, the nation is exposed to the perils of commercial disinte-
gration and consequent popular suffering, depicted
in the quotations from the advocates of armament
upon which the author bases his case. No one
imagines that fire insurance and the police are
otherwise than unremunerative expenses, unless
fire or breaches of the peace occur. The illustrations are time-worn, perhaps a little shop-worn; but
they can never be outworn, because the nature of the
provision made in police and insurance is exactly
that of armament. The new French ministry, just
constituted as I write, with the experience of the
Morocco controversy fresh in mind, affirms its faith
that a strong army and navy are the best guarantee
of peace; yet we know that its predecessor labored
for peace, and that war was averted by diplomatic
action, in which armament assuredly counted. The
War of Secession stands as a perpetual beacon
against disarmament. Never were two antagonists
less armed. A distinct preponderance of armament
on one side or the other, or such a common readiness
as would have indicated devastating hostilities,
might have held the hands of both. Certainly,
had the material superiority of the North been organized in armies and navies, there could have been
no four years of war.

In this connection it may be interesting to recall the observation of the late Mr. Carl Schurz,

.that in his wide experience of political speaking he had always found "the people" responsive to moral appeals when plainly set forth, even when the result traversed what appeared to be their self-interest. Mr. Schurz was a hater of war; but still, as he looked with emotion upon the heaped-up dead at Gettysburg, the War of Secession justified itself to his mind through the moral motive, the extinction of slavery. The two motives, moral and interested, will co-exist; but self-interest, even when recognized, does not possess the impelling power which is supplied by the sympathies, or by the sense of right and wrong. "Thrice is he armed who hath his quarrel *just*." Self-interest is also less easily perceived by the mass, because its connection with a dispute is often indirect. Bismarck *may* have engineered the wars of his day with a sole view to the material interests of Germany, but the force behind him was the passions and enthusiasm of the people.

The difference between Mr. Angell's conception and my own of the motives which move nations is illustrated by his comment upon a passage of mine quoted by him:

That extension of national authority over alien communities which is the dominant note in the world politics of to-day dignifies and enlarges each state, and each citizen that enters its fold. . . . Sentiment, imagination, aspiration, the satisfaction of the rational and moral faculties in some object better than bread alone, all must find part in a worthy motive. *Great and beneficent achievement ministers to worthier contentment than the filling of the pocket.*

Upon this Mr. Angell's comment (p. 309) is:

Have we not come to realize that this is all moonshine, and very mischievous moonshine? Let us examine it a little. A man who boasts of his possessions is not a very pleasant, admirable type, but at least his possessions are for his own use and do bring a tangible satisfaction, materially as well as sentimentally. He is the object of a certain social deference by reason of his wealth—a deference which has not a very high motive, but the outward and visible signs of which are pleasing to a vain man. But is the same in any sense true, despite Admiral Mahan, of the individual citizen of a big state as compared with the individual citizen of a small? Does any one think of paying deference to the Russian moujik because he happens to belong to one of the biggest empires territorially? Does any one think of despising an Ibsen or a Björnsen, or any educated Scandinavian, or Belgian, or Hollander, because they happen to belong to the smallest nations of Europe? The thing is absurd, and the notion is simply due to inattention, etc., etc.

This quotation, pursued, illustrates not only a dogmatic rudeness frequent in Mr. Angell's pages, but inattention or inaccuracy on his part; and also how completely his prepossession with material interest, as the great and almost sole cause of national action, dominates his power even to understand another's words. He likens the idea presented by me to the self-satisfaction of a man elated with his social position and wealth. My words, which for present convenience I have italicized, show clearly enough a wholly different ideal—that of the use of power for beneficent ends; a moral purpose, certainly. I personally am proud, as an American, of what America has accomplished in the late Spanish possessions and in the Panama Canal Zone; and if I were a Briton, I should·feel a like pride in the benefits done to India and to Egypt. I will cite, in support of this simple idea of pride in country, words of the present Mr. Charles Francis Adams, who will not be suspected of jingoism by any who know either himself or his writings. Speaking of the sanitation triumph at the Isthmus, he says, "Assuredly the world has seen nothing like it before; and, standing face to face with it, is not the American justified in a certain access of race pride?" This I conceive is precisely the gratification indicated in my words criticized by Mr. Angell—national *esprit de corps*, a moral force, the power of which is everywhere recognized.

Argument must proceed necessarily upon the recognition, illustrated by the instances cited, that with nations, as with men, absolute singleness of motive is rarely found. Mixed motive is the rule, not the exception. Mr. Angell is inclined somewhat to make merry with opponents of his thesis, because at one time they allege self-interest, at another moral motives, as the spring of impulse to war. The inconsistency of this is not in the argument, but in the complex material dealt with—human nature. Bronze is copper and bronze is tin. Nothing is gained, but much is lost, by ignoring duplexity of characteristic.

Nothing too will be gained, only time lost, by disputing the conclusion elaborated at great length by

Mr. Angell, that in the close interrelations of modern states injury done to the commercial or financial stability of one reverberates throughout the entire community, returning in due force upon the victor. His theory concerning war, and its incident armament, is founded upon the conception that both are the outcome of supposed material self-interest. Upon this basic assumption he erects the superstructure of argument that, by recognition of the fact that such self-interest does not gain by war, but loses, the motive to war and to armaments will be attenuated and ultimately will expire with the illusion which now fosters it. His premise is, I think, his own great illusion. To regard mankind, in individuals or in states, as so dominated by material self-interest that the appeal of other motives —ambition, self-respect, resentment of injustice, sympathy with the oppressed, hatred of oppression —is by it overbalanced and inoperative, is not only to misread history, but to ignore it. Almost every war of the past half-century contradicts the assertion. Nations will fight for such reasons more readily than for self-interest.

Even on the ground of self-interest only, the argument appears overstrained. That war between two great nations injures both, and that the injury is felt by the whole international community, has become a commonplace of modern political thought, testified almost yearly by the anxiety of governments to localize disputes by confining them within a given area. This anxiety is probably the largest constituent factor in the Monroe Doctrine, which seeks to localize non-American disputes by excluding their intrusion into the regions to which the doctrine applies. But when the conclusion is pressed to the point of maintaining that a disproportion between the welfare of two states may not be produced by war, to the permanent advantage of one, so that it may even advance to a position of economic supremacy, the proposition appears contestable. I had occasion several years ago to look somewhat extensively into the economical and financial conditions of Great Britain toward the end of the Napoleonic wars. They were dismal; but it is true none the less that those of the Continent were so much worse that Great Britain owed the long start which she held and kept to this cause largely, though of course not solely. A single reason rarely accounts for all the phenomena of a social order.

Great Britain owed her superiority then to the armed control of the sea, which had sheltered her commercial and industrial fabric from molestation by the enemy; while by the same means she crushed the prosperity of France, disabling her from utilizing her rich resources in the processes of commercial exchange. The latest *Encyclopædia Britannica* (1910) says:

> The commercial supremacy of England was due to a variety of causes, of which superior intelligence, in the ordinary business sense, was not the most important. Her insular position, con-

tinuity of political development, and freedom from domestic broils played an important part in bringing about a steady and continuous growth of industry and manufactures for several generations before the modern era. The great wars of the eighteenth and the beginning of the nineteenth century gave England the control of the markets of the world. When peace was restored, England had something in the nature of a monopoly.

Progress of this kind, which may not reach supremacy but simply modify the relative conditions of the states concerned, may be brought about either directly or indirectly. As the result of the war between France and Germany in 1870, Germany acquired territory and a huge indemnity. These were direct results. She received also the final impulse to national unity, consummated in the formal institution of the German Empire. *The Great Illusion* considers the territory and the indemnity to have been necessarily of doubtful benefit; but the argument is not convincing. The statement (p. 94) that prices go up as money becomes abundant is obvious, but it is difficult to understand why loans bearing interest may by good administration produce advantage to a nation—or a firm—whereas a sum bearing no interest must be a detriment. As a matter of fact, Germany was handicapped by lack of capital; due to her late entry into the industrial race and to the severe competition of neighboring rivals of longer industrial antecedents and consequent larger accumulations—of France, Great Britain, Holland, Belgium. A close and extensive student of German conditions writes of 1871, "Material enterprise of every kind was fertilized by the capital which now became loosened, and sought new and larger channels of employment."[1] The capital drawn from France could scarcely have come amiss to such conditions, though it is certain that sudden easy money caused wild speculation, with attendant disasters, as it always does.

On the other hand, German national unity has assured, throughout the countries thus confederated into one empire, the development of an economical and industrial system which, among other effects, has resulted in reducing emigration from some 200,000, in 1879, to 25,000 yearly now; although, coincident with this diminution, the population is increasing by 800,000 annually. This is indirect result. Moreover, that 25,000 outgo does not denote a surplus of unemployed, as former conditions did. On the contrary, Germany receives at certain seasons of the year a large influx of labor from surrounding districts; so that the claim has been advanced that she is now an immigrant country, notwithstanding the annual natural increase of nearly a million—aggregating fifty per cent. since 1870.

In connection with this result, from the political union of several communities previously separated, may be noted the confident assertion of *The Great Illusion* (p. 45) that enlargement of territory does not connote increase of financial prosperity. It is said, let Germany annex Holland, and not an in-

---

[1] W. H. Dawson, *The Evolution of Modern Germany*, p. 38.

dividual German or Dutchman will be a penny
the richer. There appears here the fallacy that the
administration of a large capital cannot be made
more productive proportionally than that of a smaller. Granting equal efficiency of administration, the
proposition seems to contravene experience. When
the scale of increase is as small as in this instance,
the population of the Netherlands being less than
one-tenth that of Germany, effect, even ultimate
effect, may possibly be slight. Nevertheless, it
would be there; while in the consolidation of the
German states into the German Empire, or of the
thirteen American States into the American Union,
with its subsequent expansions, the consequences
have been notorious. Both these political measures
conduced to great economic advantage, and both
were enlargements of territory. The same is true of
the unification of Italy; where also there was a first
period of great distress, followed by sustained progress.

The degree to which such consolidations are
beneficial depends upon whether they are natural—
correspond to fundamental facts—or artificial. In
the one case a nation is formed, in the other merely
a political entity—like Turkey—not homogeneous.
The effect, when real, is to extend the area of assured
peace for the communities concerned, and also to
strengthen them as competitors in the markets of
the world. Concerning Alsace-Lorraine, a much
smaller area than Holland, it has been noted that

not only did the annexation add to the industrial power of the empire by the manufacturing establishments there existing, but also that these, being brought within the industrial system of Germany, competing on equal terms, forced a higher standard upon German manufacturers as the only way to meet these new and better-equipped rivals in the home market.[1]

But it may be urged that these instances—England after the Napoleonic wars and Germany after and since the war with France—if conceded applicable at all, relate to conditions which have now passed away to return no more. Much of the argument of *The Great Illusion* turns upon the allegation that the past is in many respects so wholly past that arguments based upon its experiences are no longer valid. In his "Reply" in *The North American Review* for June, 1912, the author of the work says that I "have rejected this part of his thesis, because I revert to facts of the eighteenth and early nineteenth centuries." The opening words of this paragraph, which were in my article as first published, show that I have not overlooked this position. The years from 1870 to the present can scarcely be called the early part of the nineteenth century; but, waiving that, it is true that I do not consider that "the respective weight of factors in international development have changed radically," in

[1] Howard, *Recent Industrial Progress in Germany*, p. 29. (Houghton, Mifflin & Co., 1907.)

Mr. Angell's sense that force—armament—does not and will not play a prominent part among such factors. I hold that it does and must continue so to do. It happens that we are now in the midst —perhaps, indeed, no further than at the entrance —of an era wherein is foreshadowed clearly a future class of great issues, which in some instances have already taken concrete form. Upon these I have touched frequently in previous articles of this series. In restating the facts, I am glad to avail myself of certain phrases and expressions used in a late number of *The Spectator* (December 30, 1911) by a correspondent of the paper and criticized in the editorial columns: "The instability of the present mapping-out of the earth's surface"; "the resettlement to be accomplished"; "the capacity to govern well native populations," in whose hands vast territories now lie useless; "the capacity to bring into use material resources which lie undeveloped." "Are the British four and a half millions which alone now occupy Australia in effective occupation" of the vast continent? "Can we wonder if Germans ask themselves whether there would be fundamental iniquity if they took in hand the development of the Amazon Valley?"

The recent Morocco question was only a particular instance of this class of disputes. It must be remembered that it was not merely between France and Germany; that among its antecedents had been arrangements between France and Great Britain,

137

and France and Spain. The process of readjustments is going on before our eyes with the rapidity of a kaleidoscope; Morocco, Tripoli, Bosnia, Albania, and Macedonia, with Turkey in general—where the recent attempt at better government appears to have broken down—Persia, China, the Open Door. Our Monroe Doctrine stands, succinctly, for our intention that the like readjustments shall not take place at the expense of America; and this position may possibly be resented as a contravention of international common law. Amid all this Germany stands observant and equipped, with administrative and industrial efficiency fully demonstrated, convinced that she has not yet received her fair share of the world's activities, yet unable to find a suitable entrance to play the part to which she is equal, and, knowing herself to be, is determined to have. We know that this sentiment is prevalent. The Chancellor of the empire very recently said:

For months past we have been living, and we are living now, in an atmosphere of passion such as we perhaps have never before experienced in Germany. At the root of this feeling is the determination of Germany to make its strength and capability prevail in the world. (*The Fortnightly Review*, January, 1912, p. 147.)

Not to quote again the very similar utterance of the British Chancellor of the Exchequer already given,[1] the British head of the Admiralty, Mr. Winston Churchill, in May, 1912, two months after

[1] *Ante*, p. 89.

this article was first published (March, 1912), spoke
to the same effect as the German Chancellor:

In the circumstances amid which we find ourselves, the study
of absolute force for its own sake is perhaps not altogether un-
worthy of those who are called upon to take a share in the coun-
sels of a free people. For what lies on the other side? What
lies behind this development of force and war power? *Behind
it lies all our power to put our own characteristic and distinctive
mark upon the unfolding of the civilization of mankind.* So
long as the quality of our civilization, so long as the patriotism
and organization of our country, is sufficiently high to enable us
to produce the maximum of force at a particular point, there is
no reason why we should not hand on undiminished to those
who come after us the great heritage we have received from those
who have gone before. . . . For the rest, the best way to make
war impossible is to make victory certain.[1]

In the face of such representative utterances, it
would seem impossible to deny that something more
and higher than the mere pecuniary profit, which
is the exponent of material self-interest, enters into
the recognized motives of the nations which are
engaged now in actively exploiting the as yet unimproved regions of the world. In a reply[2] to this
present article as first published, Mr. Angell writes

The national future and welfare of France would not have
suffered one whit had Morocco passed under the administration
of Germany. Germany's real expansion, the activities by which
her people gain their livelihood, have not in the past and will no
in the future depend upon the acquisition of tropical colonie
The prosperity of Italy, if the experience of France, the mos

[1] *The Mail*, May 6, 1912.
[2] *The North American Review*, June, 1912, p. 763.

successful African colonizer in Europe, is any guide, will not be advanced by the conquest of Tripoli. . . . Both Italy and Germany are trying to follow in the African footsteps of France.

Mr. Angell says "these assertions may sound dogmatic, but they are borne out by facts from which there is no escape." They are dogmatic; and Mr. Angell is little, if not dogmatic in all things. He proceeds at once with "the facts from which there is no escape"; illustrating his statements by Tunis, which has been in French occupation for thirty years, but making no mention of the results in Algeria at the end of eighty. In this period France has so developed Algeria that from a trade of less than a million dollars it now has one of two hundred millions, five-sixths of which is with France. Such results are commonly called successful. The name Algeria is not even mentioned by him; yet as an illustration it is far better in one way than Tunis in another, considering the time element in all exploitation. *Finis coronat opus.* It happens, however, that in Tunis also the indications are as favorable as in Algeria. Since the "protectorate" in 1881, the commerce of the district has risen from eight million dollars to forty millions. As an evidence of the beneficent activities which underlie such progresses, it may be cited that in the same period the French have constructed two thousand miles of good road. What roads mean to peace and order, as well as to trade, is known by all. But granting — what I do not grant — that in such precedents there is no promise of success to similar operations in Morocco—and in Tripoli—may it not be believed that the French government and people with their experience are quite as capable of recognizing the fact as is the sole perspicacity of Mr. Norman Angell? Further, if there can be no material advantage, as Mr. Angell affirms, it is clear that persistence of effort in a line so long followed unsuccessfully must be due to some other incentive, such as that named by the British and German officials cited; namely, the ambition to bear a racial and national share in the shaping of the world's advance. To this, which is simple human nature, public and private, and not merely to the illusion, on the pre-eminence of which *The Great Illusion* bases its case, must be ascribed the repetition of the same course by France in Morocco, Italy in Tripoli, and Germany elsewhere.

In the face of the utterances quoted, and of the external conditions noted, which cover almost the whole globe outside of Europe and North America, *The Great Illusion* presses its theory of self-interest, as resulting from the economic interdependence of civilized states, to the extent of asserting a present progressive decay among them of the principle of nationality, which for the past four hundred years has been the dominant factor in the development of Europe. It urges that the interlacing of business relations, and of class interests, are sapping already the bonds of nationality. Without denying a tendency, it may be permitted to believe that the expectation of such immediate result is premature; that with so much to be done by nations, as nations, the instrument of nationality, hard won through centuries, will not be dropped as outworn. Through it in the past discordant provinces have coalesced into unities, which may be compared accurately to personalities; an analogy which the book explicitly denies. Thence has followed the beneficial effect already noted in the case of extensions of territory by consolidation. It is just as this process and the sentiment of national unity have taken place, that advance has been made or retarded. France and Great Britain, the United States, Spain in her day, have shown the benefit; Germany and Italy, the unification of which is a matter of yesterday, testify to the injury of protracted division. Prolonged absence of the sense of nationality has been the cause of the embarrassing situation in which both these states now find themselves, and consequently is also the cause of much of the disquiet of the world resultant from their seeking to retrieve their past.

It is doubtless true that an effort is being made, notably by Socialism, to break down national boundaries and to substitute for them class lines. These, *The Great Illusion* claims, would cut across and ignore national divisions. It may be that the future has in store the wreck of nationalities, and the agglomeration of peoples in the way described; but the period of transition, like that from handicraft to factory system, will be one of disorganization which will leave Europe—and America—weakened for the collision between European and Asiatic civilizations. This not only impends, but has begun, and in it the strength of Europe is the principle of nationality, developed as it now is. For it should be noted that this array of class against class imports the substitution of internal—civil—struggle for foreign, and a dissolution of social order, resembling the petty states of the middle ages which gave place to the nations of to-day. As said before, however, it seems probable that the old weapon of nationality will not be discarded in face of the remapping of the world; for the people that does so will find itself hopelessly weak in the conflict, which will remain international. Recent observers of present currents of opinion in Germany note in to-day's Socialists a very distinct departure from the ultra international and non-military standards of twenty years ago, and a movement toward nationalism. It is said also that many who vote the Socialist ticket do so as the readiest means of combating the unpopular tendencies of the government, not because of sympathy with socialistic ideals.[1] By latest advices the same result is noticeable in Italy since the war in Tripoli. The national feeling aroused affects also Socialists, and is causing socialism to recede before the spirit of nationality.

[1] *The Fortnightly Review*, January, 1912, p. 144. *The Times*, January 9, 1912.

How strong the feeling of nationality still is may
be illustrated by one of the comparisons adverse to
it used in *The Great Illusion*. It is urged that a
British noble would marry a noble woman of some
other country rather than a peasant girl of his own.
Probably; but if a working-man of British blood,
or of British citizenship, be maltreated in another
country, the noble and his class would resent the
injury with vehemence, whereas the same treatment of a foreign noble would be viewed with indifference, or at least with no more than common
human sympathy in any case of oppression. Again,
it is scarcely an exaggeration to say that Jews as a
race are not sympathetic to American feeling; yet
only a few months ago Americans have been roused
to strong national action, and still stronger excitement, by the particular conduct of a foreign state
toward a certain class of Jews, simply because they
were of American nationality, even though of foreign
birth. "As one man" is the familiar expression
for such national arousing; a stronger simile of
personality, or illustration of the strength of nationality, could scarcely be devised. In the recent
European crisis Britons and Germans have thus
stood opposed, as man to man, and the French
have stood in the same way; each people, as a person, protecting his own. It is quite true that
within each people there have been discordant
voices; but most men—individuals—have experience within their own personality of similar con-

flict of considerations, even where there is a clear predominant impulse.

In pursuit of the thesis that self-interest is the fundamental factor in international relations, and that no advantage to self-interest is obtainable by military force; or, as it is put, that "armaments exist [only] as the logical outcome of the illusion with which this book deals," *The Great Illusion* is led to disparage size, military power, and the sentiment of nationality, as elements of national well-being. Here, in passing, comment is necessary upon the remark that small, undefended states, such as Belgium and Switzerland, are equally prosperous, or more prosperous than certain large ones. These states are not wholly undefended in themselves; but their security depends upon the maintenance of the Balance of Power, which the great armed states conceive essential to their own well-being. Under the ægis of this mutual jealousy, reinforced by a moral indisposition to conscious wrong-doing, such as the wanton annexation of a weak neighbor would be, the smaller states prosper in peace, and are spared the expense of armament in great part. Their fire insurance, or war risk, is paid by other states. If a more powerful neighbor covet possession, its ambition is held in check by the motives stated, if not by others. The Turkish Empire is kept in existence by these mutual jealousies; but owing to its gross maladministration the moral deterrent from aggression has disappeared.

Piece after piece, each exceeding the area of Belgium or Holland, and much exceeding Alsace-Lorraine acquired by Germany in 1870, has been sliced away, as pretext has offered; nor is the moral sense of the world greatly shocked by processes such as now in Tripoli, which even if illegal are not inequitable, viewing the benefits which have followed invariably upon the displacing of Turkish rule. The explanation of these conditions by *The Great Illusion* (p. 44) is given otherwise, "On what does the evident security of the small state rest? On the simple fact that its conquest would assure to the conqueror *no profit*."

The German Empire is the most conspicuous instance of the recent constitution of a great nation, territorially extensive, equipped with great military force. It is also seemingly the most aggressive of the large European states; because, being narrowly circumscribed by land and by sea, owing to its geographical position and past history, it has the poorest present opportunity for expansion. From its military characteristics it is chosen by *The Great Illusion* for frequent animadversion, being cited as an instance of non-achievement of national ends as compared with smaller communities. Thus it is stated (p. 38) that Norwegian three and a half per cents stand at 102, the German three per cents at 82. As an exhibition of financial standing this has some weight, although, with the respective rates of interest, the difference is less than the first glance indicates;

but as regards national well-being as an object of government, it is not mentioned that of the Norwegian two and a half million souls 20,000 emigrate annually, of Germany's sixty-five million only 25,000, though the population increases by 800,000 annually. Comparison is instituted also between the funds of "powerless" Belgium and "powerful" Germany, 96 to 82; but the modern prosperity of Belgium antedates by nearly two generations (1815–1870) the constitution of the German Empire, with which began the great industrial advance of Germany.

Again, it is urged (p. 100) that the standard of comfort among French people is higher than among Germans, despite the industrial and commercial development of the latter, which is styled a "sensational splash." To which nation, however, shall be attributed the greater virility? to the one which, far overweighted, has done so much in a generation and at the same time increased its numbers fifty per cent., or to the one which, repressing natural growth, has thereby augmented mere material well-being? Unless a corresponding physical degeneration can be shown among Germans, there can be but one reply.

The period of distress in Germany following 1871 is attributed (pp. 95–100) freely to the indemnity of a thousand million dollars taken from France, showing, as it is claimed, the unprofitableness of indemnities; but it is not mentioned that, apart from the period of speculation unhappily excited, Germany then was passing through the transition period from an agricultural and handicraft system to the modern industrial, the same process which had been attended in other countries, notably Great Britain, with equal if not greater agitation and suffering. By writers who have not a thesis to maintain I find the indemnity considered an aid. Being so much capital, it helped the transition; which in itself was a stage toward the development that now makes Germany one of the commercial powers of the world. That in the use of the indemnity convulsions occurred, a period of speculation, does not impeach the capital, but the management. What great industrial enterprise is undertaken without an accumulation of capital assured to it? How shall a country transform its industrial system without similar aid? Again, in the same line of depreciation of Germany, it is said (p. 38, note) that in the small country Holland the wealth of the individual Dutchman averages sixteen thousand francs, while the German averages but nine thousand; but it is neglected to observe that Germany up to the middle of the last century has been an agricultural country—in 1871 three-fourths of the population was rural—capital scarce; whereas Holland, favorably situated for commerce and driven upon the outside world for employment, had long been a capitalistic country with big accumulations. A hundred years ago the Dutch did a large banking business, while the inland rural military monarchies depended upon British subsidies. It was the divisions of Germany which principally prevented her economic progress — state working against state. Consolidation into a great community gave internal peace and industrial development; but for the accumulations which constitute capital time is needed for nations as well as for an individual.

To evidence the prosperity of small countries, Norway's merchant shipping is cited as thrice that of Great Britain in proportion to population; but it is not noted that, in the same proportion, the total tonnage entered and cleared *with cargoes* in the United Kingdom is double that of Norway. That is, *in proportion to population*, there is double the commercial movement. The average size of the vessels employed is also significant of the nature of the trade, as is the proportion of sailing-vessels to steamers. The steam tonnage of Great Britain is to the sail as ten to one; while in Norway, omitting motor-boats, the two are nearly equal, steam being to sail as 1.2 to 1. So also Spain's management of the war of 1898 is compared (p. 222) with that of the United States, in order to show the superiority, even in military management, of a commercial country over one essentially military. This is, perhaps, the most extreme disregard of notorious conditions. The inefficiency of Spain is notorious in civil as well as military matters. Does any one suppose that the United States would have had a like walk-over if opposed to the military state of Germany? The trouble with Spain was not that she was military, but that she as a nation was incapable, and had been for over two hundred years.

Amid many suggestive remarks, Mr. Angell's treatment appears vitiated by failure to appreciate these and other qualifications which make against his thesis. I do not attach great importance to such oversights, except as showing the disposition common to most to press into argument all that favors a point of view, while overlooking the *per contras*. But where omission is frequent it tends to impeach either the comprehensive knowledge or the judicial fairness of the author. Instances occur not only in the book, but in the "Reply"[1] to my article as the latter was originally published. The citation of Tunis and silence as to Algeria, already noted, is paralleled by an incidental illustration in the "Reply," drawn from early Christianity.[2] To base on Simon Stylites and his admirers an assertion as to the prevalent early Christian ideas of merit, ignoring wholly the very different standards set and followed by the Apostles and Christ Himself, as well as the activities which revolutionized Europe, penetrating to all quarters, is precisely that kind of exaggeration of a part with reference to the whole in which caricature consists. Yet it is advanced as a sober and just illustration.

[1] *The North American Review*, June, 1912.
[2] *Ibid.*, p. 758.

"THE GREAT ILLUSION"

That attention has not been drawn—perhaps it has
—to these flaws in the argument of *The Great Illusion* is surprising; the more so that it seems, upon
the whole, characteristic of the general argument—
the countenance, so to say, of the work—as well as
of particular features.[1] The unquestioning acceptance of the book in so many quarters testifies either
to mental indolence to analyze, or to the fact of its
appearance at what the phrase of the day calls
a psychological moment, when the shibboleth
"Disarmament" gave free course to all who pro-
nounced it.

Insistence upon details, however, rather obscures
than elucidates, and the author's presentation of his
case suffers from this, as also, especially in the latter
part of the book, from unbecoming superciliousness
of tone. But the fundamental, decisive, error (however) is the conception that nations maintain armaments with a view to aggression in behalf of self-
interest, measured in speedy returns of dollars and
cents. This view dominates the entire book, despite
a timely caution conveyed by a prominent international banker (p. 135, note):

Though the economics of your book are unchallengeable, it
is futile for the simple reason that it deals with material interests,
and people to-day do not go to war about business or material

[1] See, in this connection, *Modern Wars and War Taxes* by W. R.
Lawson, just published. (Wm. Blackwood & Sons, Edinburgh,
1912.) This contains a criticism of the argument of *The Great
Illusion* on the financial side, which is beyond my own competency
to discuss.

151

interests. I do not know what they go to war about, but I am quite sure it is not about business.

In the past, when governments were little responsible to the people, wars were made irrespective of popular feeling from motives of advantage purely. To-day all recent history shows that governments are reluctant to go to war; but they recognize, and the people sustain them, that war may come, and that if it does it will expose the nation to vital injury to its "financial and industrial stability." This is quite different from the apprehension that the reason of an enemy for declaring war is to inflict such injury.

The causes of quarrel now are quite otherwise than the barefaced robbery which marked the career of absolute monarchs like Louis XIV., Frederick the Great, and Napoleon. The motives now are rarely simple, usually complex; but historically they have not been "to increase power and prosperity at the cost of the vanquished." Those who remember the War of Secession know how powerfully the sentiments phrased by the words "The Union" on one side, and "Independence" or "State Rights" on the other, outweighed any thought of interest. The German people rose as one man to support Bismarck, because the quarrel appealed mightily to the nascent sentiment of racial unity. Russia attacked Turkey in 1877 because of the wave of intense popular sympathy with peoples under-

going cruel oppression—a sympathy widely felt elsewhere, but in Russia only transmuted into act.
The South African war illustrated what the author
of *The Great Illusion* (*Spectator*, January 6) thinks
impracticable for the most part—namely, the protection by force of the citizens of one state in the
territory of another. The British government scarcely expected to increase its prosperity or financial stability by aggression upon the Transvaal Republic.
It stood to lose money, not to gain. The whole
question turned upon the treatment of British subjects during the interval between immigration and
naturalization; and the motive drew in not the
British Islands only, but the English race in Canada,
Australia, and New Zealand as well.

A mature consideration of the wars of the past
sixty years, and of the occasions also in which war
has seemed imminent but has been averted, will
show that the motives to war have not often been
"aggression for the sake of increasing power, and
consequently prosperity and financial well-being."
The impulses, however mistaken they are thought
by some, or actually may have been, have risen
above mere self-interest to feelings and convictions
which the argument of *The Great Illusion* does not
so much as touch. The entire conception of the
work is itself an illusion based upon a profound mis-
reading of human action. To regard the world as
governed by self-interest only is to live in a non-
existent world, an ideal world, a world possessed by

an idea much less worthy than those which mankind, to do it bare justice, persistently entertains. Yet this is the aspect under which *The Great Illusion* avowedly regards the world that now is. It matters little what the arguments are by which such a theory is advocated, when the concrete facts of history are against it.

VII

UNLESS present expectation be greatly deceived, within two decades two events will have altered very materially the territorial conditions which underlie the capacity of the United States to exert power at sea. Such changes on land influence materially the subsequent dispositions of the navy, enabling it to be more effectively utilized. One of these events will be the opening of the Panama Canal. The other, already past, has been the war with Spain, issuing in the independence of Cuba from European control and in the territorial acquisitions of the United States resulting from the war.

From a military point of view, these acquisitions have advanced the southern maritime frontier of this country from the Gulf coast to a line coincident with the south shore of Cuba, prolonged to Porto Rico; throwing into the second line the Gulf harbors, from Key West to the Mississippi. These are reduced thus to the order of purely defensive ports, instead of the primary rank of naval bases for offensive operations held by them twenty years ago—a change to which have contributed also the hydrographic difficulties of entrance and exit consequent upon the greatly increased size of battle-ships. This new condition is summarized in, and effected by, the cession of Guantanamo as a naval base; provided, of course, that due measures are taken for the security of the base, so that ships may not be tied to the defense of a position the one value of which will be that the fleet can depend upon it for supplies and repairs, yet leave it for a measurable time to its own protection, sure of finding it and its resources safe upon return.

The occupation of the Canal Zone under conditions of complete sovereignty (with qualified exceptions in the cities of Colon and Panama) may be regarded accurately, from the military point of view, as a most helpful modification of our proper coast-line, making it, by the interposition of Guantanamo, practically continuous for a fleet from the Atlantic to the Pacific. It will be continuous because possessing throughout adequate points of support— the one service which, from the military point of view, the land renders to the sea. To secure this condition, however, the Canal, like Guantanamo, must be fortified. There is, unhappily, much exaggerated talk on one side and the other as to the relative advantages of navies and fortifications for purposes of defense. Neither is secure without the other. As I have said, a fleet must be able to go away for a calculated time, with a reasonable prospect of finding its ports unsurprised, still its own, when it returns. The port must be able to spare the fleet for a similar period, confident that it can look out for itself till reinforced or supplied. The analogy is that of an army in campaign, which is crippled in movement if it has to cover its bases as well as to carry on other necessary operations.

A number of eminent citizens, more actuated by a commendable desire for peace than instructed in military considerations, not long ago put their names to a paper directed against the fortification of the Canal. In this they say, among other things, "With all the fortifications possible it is still apparent that . . . in time of war a guard of battle-ships at each of its entrances would be an absolute necessity, and equally apparent that with such a guard the fortifications would be unnecessary." I fear some naval officers, at home and abroad, dubbed in England the Blue Water School, are partly responsible for this popular impression of the need of the constant presence of battle-ships. It is precisely in order that a constant guard of battle-ships may not be necessary that fortifications are requisite. Fortifications liberate a fleet for action whenever elsewhere required; and, by preserving the Canal for use as a bridge between the two oceans, render less imperative the maintenance of a big fleet in both.

The maintenance of the Canal in effective operation is one of the large elements in the future development of sea power in the Pacific. No other nation has in the Canal the same interest of self-preservation that the United States has. Not only is this true as regards the Panama Canal, but no similar condition of dependence upon a canal exists anywhere else to near the same degree. The closest parallel is Suez, as compared with the Cape of Good Hope. Suez offers Great Britain an inside route to her great Australasian colonies, as well as to India; but the existence of the British Empire does not depend upon that route as vitally as the ability of our thickly settled Atlantic coast to come to the aid of the Pacific depends upon Panama, as compared with Magellan. This necessity is so urgent as to make the Canal, as before said, essentially a part of the coast-line of the United States.

The primary object of the Canal may have been commercial, or it may have been military. I doubt whether many of those conspicuous in its advocacy and inception analyzed to themselves which of these two obvious features was chief in their individual estimation. From either point of view, and from both, the opening of the Canal will conduce decisively to influence the development of sea power upon the Pacific. Its effect will be much the same as that of the construction of a new railroad judiciously planned, which opens out the new country through which it passes, or to which it leads, and thus not only renders it available to commerce, but by perpetual interaction of population and production increases both. More people, more wants; more people, more production. Both wants and production mean increased transportation.

This effect of the Panama Canal upon sea power will have two principal aspects—one civil, one military. The civil effect will be the more rapid peopling of the Pacific coasts of North and South America, with consequent necessary increase of commerce. The military effect will be the facility with which the navy of the United States, and that of the government controlling Canada, can pass from one side to the other, in support of either coast as needed. I say somewhat generally, but advisedly, the government controlling Canada; for, while Canada is a part of the British Empire, and therefore will receive the support of the British navy where its interests are concerned, and while Canada also, taken as a whole, is for the time present attached to the British connection, as the Thirteen Colonies were from 1732 to 1770, it is difficult, in view of current political discussions in Canada, especially those touching the question of support to the empire, not to feel that the preponderant tone there does not in this respect reflect that of Australia, New Zealand, or even of South Africa. The strong opposition in the French provinces to the government proposals for the development of a Canadian navy, the apologetic defense of the measure by the then premier, Sir Wilfrid Laurier, himself a French Canadian, in which the assertion of Canadian independence of action is more conspicuous than that of devotion to imperial interests, tend to prove a looseness of allegiance, which already simulates the independence of separation and may issue in it. After these words were written, the inference contained in them received support from the reported effect produced upon imperialistic sentiment in Great Britain by the Reciprocity agreement with the United States framed by Sir Wilfrid Laurier's government. In short, there does not appear to be between Canada and Great Britain that strong dependence of mutual interest in defense, of which the British navy is the symbol and the instrument, and which binds together the other self-governing communities. I regret this, because I believe it the advantage of the United States that Great Britain, by her relations to Canada, should be strongly committed to the naval support of the north Pacific coasts. The ultimate issue will manifestly affect the question of sea power in the Pacific, according as it involves the British navy or only a Canadian. Meantime, under present conditions, the opening of the Canal will bring the British navy six thousand miles nearer the Pacific coast of Canada.

The greatest factor of sea power in any region is the distribution and numbers of the populations, and their characteristics, as permitting the formation and maintenance of stable and efficient governments. Such stability and efficiency depend upon racial traits, the distinguishing element of which is not so much the economical efficiency of the individual citizen as his political capacity for sustained corporate action—action which, however marked by internal contentions, is in the main result homogeneous and organic. As a matter of modern history, so far, this capacity has been confined to nations of European civilization, with the recent exception of Japan. At times, it is true, great masses of men have for a period moved in unison, as by instinct, with an impetus that nothing for the moment could resist. The Huns, the Arabs, the Turks, are instances in point; but none would cite either the peoples or their governments as instances of political efficiency. At other times great personages have built up an immense sway upon their own personality alone; but the transiency of such is too proverbial for indication. The political aptitudes of the average citizen, steadied by tried political institutions, are the sole ground of ultimate national effectiveness.

The most immediate, the foremost, question of the Pacific, as affecting sea power, therefore, is the filling-up of the now partly vacant regions, our own Pacific coast, with that of the British Empire in Canada and in Australasia, by a population of European derivation. It is most desirable that such immigration should be from northern Europe, because there is found the stock temperamentally most consonant to the local institutions; but, from whencesoever coming, immigrants to all the regions named will find awaiting them settled forms of government, differing from one another much in details and somewhat in views, but all derived ultimately from the traditional ideals which we call Anglo-Saxon, to which we who have inherited them are apt to attach peculiar value and virtue. Let us not forget that the roots can be traced to the old days when the Angles and the Saxons really dwelt on the east side of the North Sea, before they found a new home in England. Thus long continuity of existence, power of development, faculty to adapt themselves to many differing circumstances of environment, as well as to absorb and to assimilate alien elements, have given a proof of their excellence more decisive than the perhaps too partial estimate of those who live under them.

That the Panama Canal can affect the rapid peopling of the American Pacific coasts is as evident as it is to be desired. That a ship-load of immigrants can be carried through relatively quiet seas direct to the Pacific ports, without the tiresome and expensive transcontinental journey by rail, will be an inestimable contribution toward overcoming the problems of distribution and of labor. It will disperse also the threatening question of Asiatic immigration to the northern Pacific coasts by filling up the ground—the only perfectly sound provision for the future. No European labor element thinks of emigrating to Asia, for the land there is already overcrowded. Were conditions reversed, Asiatic governments and working-men would feel the same objection as is now felt throughout the American Pacific to an abundant influx of laborers of wholly different traditions, who do not assimilate socially and cannot be assimilated politically. Here is no question of superiority or inferiority of race, the intrusion of which simply draws a misleading trail across the decisive reason, which is the fundamental distinctions of origin and of historical development. Already, scarcely a month after the new treaty with Japan was confirmed, the attempt has been again made thus to confuse the issue, if the quotation from a Japanese periodical is to be accepted.[1] The question is one of age-long differences, proceeding from age-long separations, producing variations of ideas which do not allow intermingling, and consequently, if admitted, are ominous of national weakness through flaws in homogeneity. The radical difference between the Oriental and the Occidental, which is constantly insisted upon, occasions incompatibility of close association in large numbers for the present, and for any near future.

The existing tendency of immigration to seek our Pacific coast is seen from the recent census, which shows that those States have progressed in population to a greater extent, proportionately, than most other parts of the country. While, however, such

[1] The *Japanese American Commercial Weekly*, quoted in the New York *Tribune*, March 27, 1911. " The present understanding with regard to Japanese immigration will be adhered to by the Japanese government with all its sincerity. Yet there is no denying the fact that the Japanese people in general are not satisfied with the arrangement. They cannot help feeling that they are not receiving fair treatment from the American government; *that the exclusion agreement stamps upon them the stigma of inferiority.*" (My Italics.)

result is indicative of tendency, it must be remembered that ratio of increase does not prove corresponding absolute gain; fifty per cent. on one thousand only equals twenty-five on two thousand. The Pacific coast States are still scantily peopled. Thus Washington contains 17 persons to the square mile, Oregon 7, California 15; whereas New York has 191 and Ohio 117.[1] The result of such conditions, where no artificial obstacle intervenes, is seen in Hawaii. These islands geographically belong to the American continent, being distant from it only 2,100 miles, whereas they are 3,400 from Japan, the nearest part of Asia; yet a plurality of the population is Japanese, from an immigration which began only forty years ago. The political—international—result may not improbably be traced in the well-known intimation of the Japanese government to that of the United States in 1897 that it could not see without concern the annexation of the islands. If the local needs which caused this condition had occurred after the opening of the Canal, the required labor could have been introduced from southern Europe,[2] which is now furnishing an excellent element to Cuba. In such case Hawaii as a naval base would have received a reinforcement of military strength, in a domiciled population of European derivation and traditions.

The Hawaiian group is an outpost of the United

[1] Census of 1910.
[2] As it is, there are over 15,000 Portuguese in the islands.

States of first importance to the security of the Pacific coast; but its situation is one of peculiar exposure. During the eighteenth century Great Britain at Gibraltar held the entrance of the Mediterranean successfully against all comers; but in the same period she twice lost Minorca, an outpost like Hawaii, because the navy was too heavily engaged in the Atlantic, and the land forces elsewhere, to afford relief. In case of the fall of Pearl Harbor, where the defense of Hawaii is concentrated, an enemy temporarily superior to the United States in local naval force would become possessed of a fortified permanent base of operations within half-steaming distance of the Pacific shore. On that shore, in furtherance of his designs, he could establish temporary depots for coaling and repairs; as Japan in the recent war did at the Elliott Islands, sixty miles from Port Arthur, then the decisive objective of her military and naval operations. Such advanced temporary positions need a permanent base not too far distant, such as the Japanese home ports Sasebo and Kure afforded the Elliott Islands, and as Pearl Harbor in the instance considered would to a navy resting upon it.

But if Pearl Harbor should hold out successfully, a superior American fleet on arrival finds there a secure base of operations, which with its own command of the water, due to its superior strength, enables it to neutralize and ultimately to overthrow any system of operations or attack resting on improvised bases and inferior fleet force. One has only to imagine the effect upon the Japanese land operations in Manchuria if Rozhestvensky had destroyed Togo's fleet and so established control of the water between Japan and Manchuria. The same line of reasoning applies to Corregidor Island, in Manila Bay, qualified by the greater distance of the Philippines from America.

The Pacific coast of America is less thickly populated, less extensively developed, than the Atlantic. Labor there is dearer, and the local coal as yet distinctly inferior for naval purposes to Eastern coal, necessitating sending fuel there. All upon which a fleet depends for vitality is less abundant, less cheap, and therefore more remote. These economical reasons, until qualified by military urgency, render expedient the maintenance of the fleet in the Atlantic. Division of it is forbidden by military considerations, in that it is too small; the half is weaker than any probable enemy. At present, not less than four months would be required for the battle-fleet to reach Pearl Harbor in effective condition. With the Canal, less than four weeks would be necessary.

These considerations affect the time that Pearl Harbor needs to hold out, and illustrate the military gain from the Canal; but they do not affect in any sense the necessity for a superior navy. Canal or no canal, if a fleet be distinctly inferior, it can protect the coast committed to its charge only to a limited degree and for a limited time, unless it can

166

reverse the balance by professional skill. The professional skill may be forthcoming—it is the affair of the commander-in-chief—but real naval security is original superiority of force, and that is the affair of the nation represented in Congress.

The great English-speaking colonies of Australia and New Zealand will be less immediately and directly affected as to populating by the Panama Canal; but its influence upon Pacific America, including Hawaii, cannot be a matter of small importance to communities which share with equal fervor the determination that their land shall be peopled by men of European antecedents. This identity of feeling on the subject of Asiatic immigration between Australia and the North American Pacific, both inheritors of the same political tradition, is certain to create political sympathies, and may drag into a common action the nations of which each forms a part. This particular determination, in the midst of that recent prevalent unrest which is called the Awakening of the East, is probably the very largest factor in the future of the Pacific, and one which eventually will draw in most of the West-European nations in support of their present possessions in the East. Immediately north of Australia, barricading it, as it were, from west to east, is a veritable Caribbean of European tropical possessions—Sumatra, Java, to New Guinea—distributed between Germany, Great Britain, and Holland; while immediately north of them again come the

Philippines under American administration. It is needless to say that support to such distant dependencies means military sea power; but it is less obvious, until heeded, that the tendency will impart a common object—a solidarity of interest—which may go far toward composing present rivalries and jealousies in Europe. To none, however, can this interest be so vital as to Great Britain, because Australasia is not to her a dominion over alien races, as India is, and as are most European possessions in the East. The Australians and New-Zealanders are her own flesh and blood; and, should the question of support to them arise, the Panama Canal offers an alternative route not greatly longer to eastern Australia, and shorter by over twelve hundred miles to New Zealand. It is, however, in the developed power of Pacific America, including Canada, that Australia in the future will find the great significance of the Panama Canal.

The question of immigration is now engaging the aroused attention of the new "Labor" government in Australia. Equally with our own Pacific slope, peopling will be there a large influence in the sea power of the Pacific. The question is felt to be urgent, because much of the vast territory of Australia is empty. Excluding aborigines, the population is less than two to the square mile. In New Zealand the proportion is only nine. The huge tropical district in Australia known as the Northern Territory, with an area of 523,620 square miles, contains but one thousand whites. After a seeming attempt to coddle the labor question, to sustain high wages by discouraging immigration, Australia is awaking to the untenable and perilous situation in which a people is placed when seeking to hold a great inheritance which they neither occupy nor by numbers can develop. It matters not for the moment whence the danger may come. From some quarter it will, soon or late—probably soon. Overcrowded millions not far off will not look indefinitely upon open pastures denied them only by a claim of pre-emption. An abundant population in possession is at once a reason and a force.

To those who do not follow passing events which seem remote from ourselves, it should be of interest to recall—for it is cognate to our subject—that the still recent year 1910 witnessed the visit to Australia and New Zealand of Lord Kitchener, the greatest military organizer and most distinguished British soldier now in active service. The object desired by the colonial governments was that a scheme of defense based upon territory, population, and resources should be devised, after personal examination, by the man who, as commander-in-chief in India, had recast comprehensively the military system upon which rests the defense of three hundred millions of people, and of a territory which in area is a continent. The broad details of his recommendations have been made known through the press, but are not here material. It is sufficient to say that, since his departure, a new "Labor" government of the commonwealth has come into power, and in all decisive particulars has adopted his plan. The nature of the popular preponderance behind this government is sufficiently indicated by the name—Labor. It is the first since the organization of the Commonwealth—the union of the several states—that has possessed a homogeneous working majority; and it is significant of the future that the first care of a labor ministry has been to provide an efficient military organization, and to entertain measures for the development of a railway system which shall minister not only to economical development, but to national military security.

In introducing the necessary legislation the Minister of Defense, after fully adopting Lord Kitchener's scheme, "attacked those who placed faith in arbitration." He declared "that Australia would refuse to arbitrate about Asiatic exclusion, and must be prepared to maintain its own laws against attack. If any one asked why the Labor party was especially keen on military matters, the answer was that the proposed social and industrial reforms of the party required freedom from disturbance, which they must effectively secure."[1] In the Australian press of the following day, quoted in telegrams to the London *Times*, no dissent from this speech is noted. "The reception accorded to the bill indicates a complete severance of the question from party

[1] *The Mail* (tri-weekly London *Times*), August 19, 1910.

politics. It is assured of an untroubled passage through both houses."[1]

It is not difficult here to note the identity of tone with that of the Pacific slope of the United States and of Canada, to the frequent embarrassment of both central governments. It is increasing in imperativeness in British Columbia, is extending thence eastward to Alberta and Saskatchewan, and is felt even as far as Winnipeg. Use the phrase "national honor," "vital interests," or what you will, there are popular sentiments and determinations which defy every argument but force. It is the failure to note these which vitiates much of the argument for arbitration. Such sentiments, on both sides, are large factors to be taken into account in the forecast of the future of sea power in an ocean one of whose shores is Asiatic, the other European in derivation.

The Panama Canal will tend to link the several English-speaking communities affected by these feelings, and to emphasize their solidarity; not least by the greater nearness which it will give the North American districts to the more thickly settled, and consequently more powerful, Atlantic regions with which they are politically united. Debatable ground, undeveloped occupation, such as exists in them all, is from this particular point of view an especial source of weakness. In none of them, and especially in Australia and New Zealand, is the population proportionate to the soil. The garrison is not

[1] *The Mail,* August 22, 1910,

commensurate to the extent of the walls. Hence immigration becomes a pressing question; and in Australia radical land legislation to break up huge unimproved holdings, and so to facilitate agricultural immigration, is a prominent feature in prospective legislation.

This state of things is a matter of consummate moment, and will compel the sympathy of American Pacific communities with peoples who discern a common danger, and who share a common political tradition. This weakness explains also the evident closer attachment of Australasia than of Canada to the mother-country. Not only is there no alien element, like the French Canadian, but there is far greater exposure and sense of dependence, such as our own ancestors felt when Canada was French. Here enters the sea power of Great Britain into the Pacific with an urgency even greater than that of commercial gain. It is there a question of keeping her own. So far as Australia is weak in numbers, she is proportionately dependent upon power at sea to prevent those numbers from having to encounter overwhelming odds on shore. In this, her case resembles that of the British Islands themselves. She has shown sense of that dependence by the adoption of naval measures much more virile than those which in Canada are meeting opposition; but at best her resources are not sufficient, and dependence on the mother-country will be for a long time inevitable.

The appositeness of these preparations of Australia—and of New Zealand—has been emphasized recently by the resolute persistence of Germany in augmenting materially her naval programme. The latest measures voted, May, 1912, add three heavy battle-ships to the projected total, making forty-one in all; raise the number in active commission from sixteen to twenty-five; and increase the personnel by over fifteen thousand men, which when realized will give a total of over seventy-five thousand.

Lord Kitchener is quoted[1] as saying: "It is an axiom of the British government that the existence of the empire depends primarily upon the maintenance of adequate and efficient naval forces. As long as this condition is fulfilled, and as long as British superiority at sea is assured, then it is an accepted principle that no British dominion can be successfully and permanently conquered by an organized invasion from oversea." The remark was addressed to Australia specifically, and accompanied with the admonition that a navy has many preoccupations; that it may not be able immediately to repair to a distant scene of action; and that therefore the provision of local defense, both by forts and mobile troops, is the correlative of naval defense. This impedes and delays an invader, lessens his advance and the injury possible, and so expedites and diminishes the task of the navy, when this, having established preponderance elsewhere, is able

[1] *The Mail*, April 18, 1910.

to appear in force upon the distant waters of a remote dependency.

It will be recognized that the result here stated is that predicated from the arrival of a superior American fleet at Hawaii. What is true of a territory so distant from Great Britain as Australia is doubly true of the relations of the American navy to its two coasts, the Pacific and the Atlantic, of which the Gulf coast in this connection may be regarded accurately as an extension. In the eye of the navy the three are parts of one whole, of which the link, the neck of the body, will be the Canal—as Australia is not merely a remote dependency, but a living member of the British Empire. There is, however, a vital difference between a member and the trunk. Amputation of the one may consist with continued life, as Great Britain survived the loss of her Amercan colonies; but the mutilation of the trunk means, at the best, life thenceforward on a lower plane of vigor.

The military, or strategic, significance of the Panama Canal, therefore, is that it will be the most vital chord in that system of transference by which the navy of the United States can come promptly to the support on either coast of the local defenses; which it is to be presumed will be organized as Australia contemplates, even though the presumption be over-sanguine, in view of our national ignorant self-complacency. With a competent navy, and with the Panama Canal secured, not merely as to tenure, but with guns of such range as to insure deployment in the open sea at either end—a necessary condition of all sea-coast fortification—invasion will not be attempted, for it can lead to no adequate results.

It is continually asserted that no invasion of the United States will ever be attempted, because conquest is not possible. Conquest of a fully populated territory is not probable; but dismemberment, such as the instance of France deprived of Alsace and Lorraine by Germany, or more recently of Bosnia and Herzegovina taken from Turkey by Austria, is possible. In the latter case, Turkey, Russia, and all Europe were silenced by arms two years ago. What is more within the scope of possibility is the exaction from defeat of terms well-nigh unendurable. An Australian[1] has recently said, "We recognize well that if the British navy be once overthrown, a condition of peace will be that its present power shall not be restored." *Vae victis.* Defeat of the American navy, followed by a prolonged tenure of parts of American territory, which would then be feasible, might be followed by a demand to give up the Monroe Doctrine, to abandon Panama, to admit immigration to which either our government or a large part of our population objects, and on no account to attempt the re-establishment of a military or naval force which could redeem such consequences. So Rome forever disabled Carthage in the conflict between those two alien and rival civilizations.

[1] Sir George Reid, the High Commissioner for Australia in Great Britain, *The Mail*, July 8, 1910.

So much for national defense, the first of military objects because it is the foundation on which national action securely depends. But in actual warfare the defensive in itself is ineffectual, and useful only as the basis from which the offensive, technically so styled, is exerted. So in a general scheme of national policy, assured security at home is above all valuable by enabling a government to be effectively firm and influential in its support of its external commercial interests, of its necessary policies, and of its citizens abroad. The frequent impatient disclaimer of such interests, of such policies, and of the necessity of power—not necessarily the use of force—to insure them, simply ignores, not the past only, but current contemporary history. The French Minister for Foreign Affairs has spoken recently, in a public utterance, of "the ever-increasing part which diplomacy is called upon to play in the commercial activity of nations." American enterprise and American capital are seeking everywhere lawful outlets and employments. There are many competitors from many other nations; and all governments make it now part of their business to insist on the lawful admission of their own people, and in many cases to obstruct the intrusion of rivals. The Pacific in its broad extent and upon its coasts contains some of the most critical, because least settled, of these questions. Besides the ancient Asiatic peoples on its western shores, all the principal European states possess therein colonies and naval

stations; consequently are possible parties to the as
yet remote final adjustments. America in the Philippines has in the Pacific that which she may not call
her own possession, but has recognized as her especial
charge.

The Panama Canal will be the gateway to the
Eastern Pacific, as Suez is to the Western. It will
lie in territory over which the United States has
jurisdiction as complete, except in the cities of Colon
and Panama, as over its other national domains.
It is entitled to protection equally with all others;
and far more than most, not on its own account
chiefly, but because of its vital consequence to all
three coasts, and to their communications. This
consequence rests upon its being the only link between them, enabling the United States to concen-
trate the fleet with the greatest rapidity upon any
threatened or desired point. In nothing is general
importance, national importance, as contrasted with
local, more signally illustrated than it is in the
Canal and in the navy. Nowhere are considerations
of local advantage more out of place and discred-
itable than in dealing with these two great factors
of national security and dignity. Their combined
effect, so essential to defense, is no less important to
the influence of the country throughout the Pacific
Ocean. I say, influence; not supremacy, a word which
my whole tone of thought rejects. How large a part
China, for instance, has played in our international
policy of the last decade is easy to recall; nor is there

room to deny our interest in her, or her look toward us and toward others at the present moment. Even in Great Britain, by formal treaty the ally of Japan, and now in *entente* with Russia, anxiety concerning the future in Korea and Manchuria is shown, and not without cause.

In brief conclusion, Sea Power, like other elements of national strength, depends ultimately upon population—upon its numbers and its characteristics. The great effect of the Panama Canal will be the indefinite strengthening of Anglo-Saxon institutions upon the northeast shores of the Pacific, from Alaska to Mexico, by increase of inhabitants and consequent increases of shipping and commerce. To this will contribute that portion of present and future local production in the North American continent which will find cheaper access to the Atlantic by the Canal than by the existing transcontinental or Great Lakes routes. An official of the Canadian Pacific Railway has stated recently, before the London Chamber of Commerce, that even now British manufactures find their way to British Columbia by the Suez Canal; how much more by Panama, when that canal becomes available! If manufactures, then immigrants; and equally, for it is facility of transportation which determines both. The effect, he estimated, would extend inland to the middle of Saskatchewan, seven or eight hundred miles from the Pacific coast; and his plea was for British immigration as well as for British trade, to offset the known inrush from the western part of the United States. Whether American or English, there will be increase of European population. This development of the northeast Pacific will have its correlative in the distant southwest, in the kindred commonwealths of Australia and New Zealand; the effect of the Canal upon these being not direct, but reflected from the increased political force and military potentiality of communities in sympathy with them on the decisive question of immigration. The result will be to Europeanize these great districts; in the broad sense which recognizes the European derivation of American populations. The Western Pacific will remain Asiatic, as it should.

The question awaiting and approaching solution is the line of demarcation between the Asiatic and European elements in the Pacific. The considerations advanced appear to indicate that it will be that joining Puget Sound and Vancouver with Australia. It is traced roughly through intervening points, of which Hawaii and Samoa are the most conspicuous; but there are outposts of the European and American tenure in positions like the Marshall and Caroline Islands, Guam, Hongkong, Kiao Chau, and others, just as there are now European possessions in the Caribbean Sea, in Bermuda, in Halifax, remains of past conditions. The extensive district north of Australia, the islands of Sumatra, Java, Borneo, New Guinea, and others, while Asiatic in population, are, like India, European in political control.

During the period of adjustment, needed for the development of Pacific America and Australasia, naval power, the military representative of sea power, will be determinative. The interests herein of Great Britain and of the United States are preponderant and coincident. By force of past history and present possessions the final decision of this momentous question will depend chiefly upon them, if concurring. Meantime, and because of this, the American navy should be second to none but the British. To this the American may properly cede superiority, because to the British Islands naval power is vital in a sense in which it is not to the United States.

VIII

In approaching the question of fortifying the Panama Canal it is well to remember at once that the Canal Zone, with the qualified exceptions of the cities of Colon and Panama, is United States territory. In the treaty of cession there is a clause providing for the extradition of offenders between the Zone and the Republic of Panama. Being, therefore, territory rather than property, to ask guarantees of neutrality from foreign states is to constitute a kind of protectorate over ourselves. This would contravene also our traditional policies, by inviting the participation of non-American states in the assuring of American conditions; a lapse the more grievous when it is remembered that the Zone has become ours by acquisition from another American commonwealth. How strenuously the nation resented co-partnership in the affairs of the Isthmus is testified by the whole history of the Clayton-Bulwer Treaty; a resentment which verged so closely on bitterness during the final twenty years of the discussion as to be a warning against any reconstitution of similar conditions. We should have perpetual discussions with foreign nations about American affairs, such as have enlivened, and not sweetened, much of Great Britain's occupancy of Egypt.

It is also to be remembered that, besides being American soil, the Panama Canal Zone cannot be looked upon as an isolated position such as the Philippines. The loss of the Philippines by war, as a material result, would be to us like the loss of a little finger, perhaps of a single joint of it. The Philippines to us are less a property than a charge. The Canal Zone, on the contrary, must be regarded in its geographical and military relations—the two adjectives are in this connection almost identical —to the United States as a whole and to other specific American stations.

In discussing the question of the advisability of fortifying the Zone, and especially the two entrances, or exits, it is to be said at once that I represent only myself. I speak for the opinions of no one else. I am entirely aware that there is a school of naval opinion, respectable in numbers as in other qualities, though I believe a minority, which so subordinates the question of fortification to that of the numbers of the fleet as to assert practically the needlessness of fortification. I myself have been taxed by a prominent exponent of this school in Great Britain with dereliction from my own position as an advocate of sea power, because of my strong insistence upon the general necessity for fortified seaports, as es-

sential to the fleet's freedom of movement. Whatever dereliction there may seem to have been was
coincident with the first formulation of my views
upon sea power. Full twenty years ago I wrote,
and I repeat with the conviction of the years since
past: "Navies do not dispense with fortifications
nor with armies; but, when wisely handled, they may
save their country the strain which comes when
these have to be called into play."[1]

Upon the general question of sea-coast fortification, as distinct from the special question of fortifying the Panama Canal, the reasons why fortification
is an essential complement of a navy are twofold.
Sea-coast fortification supplies a navy with fortified
bases, strictly analogous to the fortresses which are
the home bases, or to the temporarily fortified positions, which are the advanced bases, of an army in
campaign. To argue the advantage—nay, the need—
of these would be to discuss military art from its
foundation. It is sufficient to say that all military
history testifies to it. One of the most distinguished of
the opponents of the first Napoleon said, "An army
which has to insure the protection of unfortified bases
is crippled in all its movements." In a naval campaign the navy is the mobile army in the field.
It, too, requires bases concerning the security of
which it need feel no apprehension.

The second office of sea-coast fortification is that

[1] *The Influence of Sea Power Upon the French Revolution and
Empire.* Vol. I, p. 341.

of simple protection. It is gravely argued that, because a recent international stipulation provides that unfortified seaports shall not be bombarded, therefore protection is unnecessary and even inexpedient. I presume the stipulation applies to all forms of military protection—submarine-mines, and so forth; and it is a natural deduction that it similarly applies to any form of military force opposing possession. That is, a hostile navy, or expedition, may not bombard an unprotected port, but it may take possession of it; and if the act be resisted, or recovery attempted, all military rights revive— bombardment included, if necessary. If this be so, and it seems strictly logical, the neglect to fortify can apply only to those points the occupation of which by an enemy is a matter of indifference to the country. There doubtless are many such. It is the province of a scheme of sea-coast fortification under joint army and navy supervision to determine which these are, and the relative claims of those where defense is needed. An undefended neutrality of the Canal Zone would forbid an enemy's bombarding; but it would not deter him from occupying if at war with the United States, because the position is too valuable not to be secured, if possible.

To apply these general considerations to the specific case of the Panama Canal. What will be the value of the Canal to the United States, and, incidentally, to the United States navy? Primarily, and above all, it will be the most important link in

the line of communications between our Atlantic
and Pacific coasts. There is throughout the whole
length and extension of our sea-coast, from Maine
to Puget Sound, no single position or reach of water
comparable to Panama in this respect. Communications, the free access to an army to its source of
supplies—or, rather, the free passage of supplies to
it—and the ability of one part of the army to reach
the other for material support, or of the whole to
move to any particular point of a theater of war—
communications, in this sense, are the most important factor in war. Communications dominate
war in all its aspects. On a battle-field the connection of the several divisions of an army must be
such that an enemy cannot break through. Advancing in campaign, the relations of army corps to
each other must be such that they can unite before
the enemy attacks either in force. Concentration,
of which we hear so much, and so justly, means
simply communications so preserved as to enable
the whole to live and the parts to unite betimes.

What is the meaning of the well-known urgency
of the Pacific coast population that the government
divide the battle-fleet, sending one-half to that coast?
This would be the most entirely suicidal act that could
be contemplated. The wish proceeds from an uneasy
sense that the whole may not be able to reach the
Pacific betimes, in case of the sudden outbreak of a
Pacific war. In other words, they are uneasy about
the communications, although very possibly the word

in that sense is as foreign to them as is any reasoned knowledge of warfare. The absence of such knowledge is evident in this desire for division, which ignores the recent destruction in detail of the Russian navy in the war with Japan.

The question of fortifying the Canal, therefore, is the question of preserving an essential line of naval communications. But, it will be replied, you beg the question; the navy will protect its own communications, the Canal not least. Will, then, the navy be tied to the Canal, or will it protect it by a big detachment, by dividing its numbers while the bulk of the fleet goes to some other assigned duty? Yes, it is replied, the money spent for fortifications, which are immobile, will be given to ships, which, though mobile, will remain for defense of the Canal, and yet, if required, can go to reinforce the fleet. Just so; if required, they will go away. One advantage of fortifications is that, being established in moments of calm consideration, they cannot be moved in moments of real or panicky pressure. A primary charge of Nelson for the naval defense of Great Britain, when invasion was feared, was that the "block ships," floating forts, established on a reasoned scheme, should on no account be moved in an apparent emergency. He recognized the danger which permanent fortification obviates. Moreover, to use active vessels for stationary defence is to lock up mobile force in an inferior effort. "To decrease our cruisers at sea by commissioning vessels for

harbor defense," said St. Vincent, second only to
Nelson, "will be a step that can lead only to our
ruin."

It is often argued that, because an enemy intend-
ing the invasion of a country situated as the United
States is must primarily possess a competent navy,
therefore, the best defense against invasion on either
large or small scale is a mobile navy. This is perfectly
true, and applies with equal or greater force to the
maintenance of oversea dependencies, such as Hawaii,
Guantanamo, the Philippines, and the Canal Zone. A
navy at least equal to that of the enemy is essential
to their preservation, but it does not follow that the
navy must be immediately present at either or all.
A navy does not protect by local presence, but by
action upon the lines of communication; that is,
upon the sea. Hence fallacy enters with the further
assertion that all money spent on fortifications had
better be spent on ships. The question is one of
proportion. Coast fortification may be pushed, at
times has been pushed, to an extravagant extent.
But for the defense of points the tenure of which is
essential to military operations—the operations of a
fleet—fixed works are better than floating because
they secure the same aggregate gun defense at much
less cost; or, if you prefer it so stated, much greater
defensive strength for the same cost. In addition
to the fact that they cannot be moved under popular
apprehension,—such as kept the Flying Squadron in
Hampton Roads during the war with Spain, a meas-

ure which would have cost the country dear with a more active enemy,—guns in forts cost far less, under normal conditions, than those in ships. Forts need no floating power, no motive machinery, no long storage of fuel. Moreover, they are less vulnerable; for the solidity of the ground permits the accumulation of armor or other protective covering, and they have not to dread the submarine or the floating mine.

Guns on board ships are also necessarily massed within the length of the ship, presenting a concentrated target; whereas on shore they may be dispersed indefinitely, and largely concealed, which is the modern practice. For such reasons, while vessels have usually been able to run by forts through an *unobstructed* channel, the same amount of artillery in ships has rarely been able to stand up against forts. Even with superior fire, ships have been able to dominate landworks only under peculiar conditions, which the all-big-gun ship does not possess; namely, the conditions of very rapid fire from very numerous pieces at very close range. No one is going to take a ten-million-dollar battle-ship over an unexplored mine-field to get near the same number of guns ashore; nor will it be attempted to engage at a distance, because the ship is much more open to fatal injury by a chance shot than a landwork is. Besides the two Japanese battle-ships destroyed by Russian mines, a third, the *Asahi*, very narrowly escaped being struck by a shell which might well have caused serious injury. The forts were not seriously hurt by naval bombardment; and it may profitably be remembered that the work of repairing the battle-ships injured by the first torpedo attack was carried on in Port Arthur during the period in which the Japanese naval bombardments occurred.

Granting, then, that the United States intends to make sure of the use of the Canal in war, fortification will insure that especial end more cheaply, with less danger of losing the position, than the same amount of money expended in war-ships, unless there are abnormal peculiarities of the ground of which I have not heard. President Taft, in a public speech, has stated that the estimated cost is $12,000,-000—less than that of two completed battle-ships. It is to be taken for granted that the Board of Fortification, checked as it should be by a naval representation, will not pile Ossa on Pelion in needless multiplication of defenses, but will have a due regard to the fundamental fact that the defenses exist for the Canal, and not the Canal for the sake of being defended. That is, it will be remembered that from the broad military point of view, which includes the entire military establishment of the country as a composite whole—army, navy, coast defense—the value of the Canal is not its impregnability as a position, but its usefulness to the navy as the offensive defender of the whole national coast-line—Atlantic, Gulf, and Pacific.

Some fifteen or twenty years ago the then senior

British naval officer at Gibraltar said to me, laughing: "The army fellows boast that they have so fixed things that the place cannot be taken; but I tell them, what does it matter whether Gibraltar be taken or not, unless its docks, stores, and anchorage are equally secured for the fleet?" Nothing whatever; it would be a barren possession. Yet its history from its capture in 1704, then merely for a naval base, to the present day has demonstrated that the fortified impregnability of the Rock of Gibraltar has been a main factor in that supremacy of the British navy in the Mediterranean which has largely shaped modern history. The Panama Canal has a still closer relation to the Pacific, the history of which is yet to make.

Mere defense is a poor thing; it is chiefly as conducive to liberating the offensive arm that it has military value. If ports are reasonably secure, the navy acts freely; if not, or if the people think not, a clamor will arise, as during our war with Spain, for ships to be scattered everywhere to defend; emasculating or neutralizing the fleet. The Panama Canal duly fortified will be a defensive provision which will permit the American navy to leave it to itself for a measurable period—as the British fleet historically has left Gibraltar and Malta. It also will enable the fleet to issue upon either ocean in effective order. It is to be remembered that one of the requirements of a fortified port is that it should cover the fleet while going out, through the always

WHY FORTIFY THE PANAMA CANAL?

critical period during which it has to pass from the
order imposed by the narrowness of a channelway
to that which it wishes to assume for action. This
corresponds to the deployment of an army from
the relatively narrow roads, over which it has been
advancing, into the alignments of an established
order of battle that may extend over many features
of country impracticable for marching. In column,
undeployed, the fleet, if handicapped by the ground,
as is usual near ports, has but partial use of its guns,
and the rear vessels support the leaders imperfectly,
or not at all. Under such circumstances an equal
enemy is for the moment superior, and momentary
superiority properly improved becomes permanent.
This is the art of war in a nutshell. Guns on shore
either will prevent the enemy from improving such
an opportunity, or at least will impose such caution
and such distant fire as greatly to reduce it. No
fleet will readily encounter shore guns when it
expects immediately afterward to meet an equal
of its own kind.

This consideration applies also in measure to the
maintenance of the neutrality of the Canal, which
the United States guarantees. Our possession ex-
tends over the conventional three-mile limit to sea-
ward. Within that distance the United States is
responsible to any belligerent which may be attacked there by its opponent. We may, of course,
"take it out of" the aggressor by any retaliation we
please, up to and including making war upon him;

but our responsibility to the sufferer is not thereby removed. In these days of excessive long range the temptation to a fleet lying outside the three-mile limit to open upon one changing its array within it may transcend control. The knowledge that in such case shore guns could open would be a deterrent. Men are too prompt to assume scrupulous respect for neutrality. That it will be disregarded is—has been—asserted to be "unthinkable." As a matter of fact, the temptation to shave the line exists in this as it does in matters of more strictly legal obligation; and it is well known what shaving the line too often ends in. Under temptation, neutrality undefended has fared no better. A fleet lying at anchor may be respected; but, when coming out, is a change of order to one for battle to be considered a belligerent act justifying attack? How will it appear to the judgment of the outside commander? Certainly the one inside will not cross the three-mile limit undeployed, if he can manœuver within. At this moment the proposed fortification of Flushing by Holland is accounted for in the public opinion of Europe only by the purpose of preventing a British force, naval or military, from proceeding up the Scheldt, the entrance of which would thus be commanded. This would close the easiest route by which Great Britain could maintain the neutrality of Belgium, as she is bound by guarantee to do.

It has been said that the Panama Canal Zone is not to be looked upon as isolated, but in its relations to other American conditions. This is true in any scheme of coast defense, and emphatically in that of a country with two sea frontiers as widely separated from each other as our Atlantic and Pacific. The primary value of Panama is that already indicated, of a connecting-link. In this sense it falls rather under the head of defensive ports; the preservation of the Isthmus as a link being precedent in importance to operations based upon it as a position. It is only in case of war simultaneously in both oceans that it would receive peculiar offensive value. As an offensive base Panama is less eligible than Guantanamo, which is at present one of the most valuable strictly military positions in the possession of the United States. New York, Guantanamo, and the Canal, analyzed severally and collectively from the military point of view, present a very notable triad of positions. Should a nation having a navy somewhat superior to the American desire, in case of war, to obtain the Isthmus—a wish in no wise "unthinkable," seeing the value of the position, seeing also that Great Britain did seize and still retains Gibraltar, and Germany did compel the cession of Kiao Chau— if the Canal Zone be properly fortified it will be better defended by an inferior navy at Guantanamo than at the Isthmus; because Guantanamo as a position flanks all communications to the Isthmus through the Caribbean Sea, while also covering those of the Gulf of Mexico and, in measure, those of the

Atlantic coast. In a foreign attempt to reduce the Canal Zone, an inferior American fleet at the Isthmus would be like the Russian at Port Arthur, where, being retained close to the central effort of the war, the Japanese main fleet readily checked Russian naval movements by occupying a position in which it at the same time covered the operations and communications of the Japanese armies in Manchuria and before Port Arthur. At Guantanamo an equivalent American fleet would be as the Russian if it had been concentrated at Vladivostok. There the Japanese navy could have checked the threat to Japanese sea communications only by removing bodily to the neighborhood of the port, thus exposing the maritime communications of their armies to harassment by cruisers acting singly or in small squadrons.

It remains true, however, that while such would be the better position for a navy slightly inferior, permanent inferiority means inevitably ultimate defeat, which fortification can only delay. Gibraltar itself was saved only by the British navy maintaining its communications; but its fortifications obtained time to act for the navy, handicapped by many other calls to many other quarters, in some of which it was often inferior. Not five years have elapsed since the "unthinkable"—in the eyes of many—has occurred in Europe; a treaty directly disregarded on the dictates of a pressing emergency and discussion of the action refused. If the United States desires peace with security—security for its outlying possessions like the Canal Zone, and for great national policies like the Monroe Doctrine—it must have a navy second to none but that of Great Britain; to rival which is inexpedient, because for many reasons unnecessary.

IX

In military activities the question of the utilization of the armed forces is the most critical and the most vital that confronts a nation. Utilization in war is the final stage of a progress which begins with the drill-ground, where the raw recruit is fashioned into the finished soldier, and with the workshops where crude material is converted into weapons of war. Utilization presupposes all the successive processes of organization and equipment; whereby, step by step, out of individual men are built up huge military units, army and army corps, battle-fleet and battle-ship, as individual in their power of intelligent corporate action as is the one man in his single existence. Thus, assuming the foundations upon which action rests, the directing authority dismisses them out of mind, concentrating attention purely upon the problem how best *to use* those entities which organization and equipment have supplied. It is to a similar concentration I would here invite readers, asking them also to dismiss from their minds, as not under consideration, all thought of the material of war, of the antecedent processes by which a national fleet or national army is built up; to accept each and both as being ready, with only the one question remaining: how they, or either of them, is *to be used* to the best advantage in war?

The methods by which this result is to be reached are divided naturally under three heads. These, in the order of time sequence, are Movement, Strategy, and Tactics. The first of these comprises not only motion, but all the dispositions for marches and transportation of supplies which make possible the transference of armies over ground, in advance or in retreat. This function of moving armies and their trains has received the technical name Logistics. Various derivations have been assigned for this term; the one now generally accepted is from a Greek word, the root idea of which is "calculation." It is not necessary to enlarge upon the complications of detail involved in moving huge bodies of men, with their supply-trains, by calculated progress, stage by stage; including each day's march, each day's halt, each day's meals, over roads in any case relatively narrow. All this may be assumed, or left to the imagination. But it should be observed that the special characteristic of this class of operations is movement, pure and simple. The movement, it is true, is minutely organized in many intricate particulars, and therefore is truly a work of military art; but withal it is not accompanied by those particular directive ideas which in strategy and tactics make movement subordinate to action, in which movement is in itself merely contributory. In short, in logistics movement is the principal; whereas in strategy and tactics it is only an agent.

In sea warfare the analogue of logistics is found, but much simplified in conception by that quality which is the distinguishing characteristic of sea forces—mobility. Mobility facilitates supply, as it does the movement of the fleet itself. The narrow strip of marching surface afforded even by the greatest highways is superseded by the broad bosom of the deep. The ocean presents no natural impediments, few obstacles. Each ship carries stores for weeks; and at night there is no halt, no wait for food-supplies. The vessels move straight on for their goal with unwearied crews. The necessary train of supply-ships, repair-vessels, colliers, all have mobility like to that of the fleet itself. But there remains a counterbalancing factor affecting the question of sea logistics: that of sustained movement and maintenance during a campaign. Fleets more often than not operate remote from home. Consequently, the chief items of supply must traverse long sea distances, under conditions of exposure exceeding the corresponding chain of supplies of an army, which in their approach are secured in large measure by the interposition of the army itself between them and the enemy; a safeguard expressively phrased in the words "covering the communications." In such case land communications may suffer by a raid, unexpectedly and momentarily; but raids by land are restricted in time and space by the imperfect mobility inherent in land conditions, whereas the mobility which is the prerogative of the water makes sea communications much more liable to successful harassment.

It will be recognized, therefore, that the determining the places of rendezvous for coal and other supplies, the protection of the routes, the whole question of keeping the holds and coal-bunkers full, and the several ships in best steaming condition, is a big administrative calculation and co-ordination, which is an instance of logistics because it directly affects the fleet's power of action. Nelson, by diligent watchfulness, always during his last great campaign had his ships stored full for three months; usually for five. That is, the movement of his fleet, wherever he would, was assured for those periods. Wrote a contemporary to him:

You have extended the powers of human action. After an unremitting cruise of two long years in the Gulf of Lyons, to have proceeded, *without going into port*, to Alexandria [in Egypt], from Alexandria to the West Indies, from the West Indies back again to Gibraltar; to have kept your ships afloat, your rigging standing, and your crews in health and spirits, is an effort such as never was realized in former times. You have protected us for two long years, and you saved the West Indies by only a few days.

This was an achievement of logistics, of movement constant and unimpaired, because of diligent prevision. No fighting; yet it underlay Trafalgar.

Yet it is very different from the battle Trafalgar, which illustrates tactics; different also from the various movements of the British and hostile fleets in the half-year before Trafalgar, in which there was abundance of motion directed toward specific points and with specific aims, covering both the Atlantic and the Mediterranean. The general conceptions underlying such specific aims are known as strategy; the movement of ships in furthering them was merely a contributory agent, which resulted in bringing the fleet to the scene of action. In like manner the movement of the ships in the battle was merely contributory, to carry out the tactical conception of the method of attack.

From the outline sketch of logistics here presented it is evident that it is an immense administrative function, covering many details and requiring much system and prevision, justifying the derivation from "calculation." In management, however, it is somewhat deliberate, and should fall mainly upon men subordinate in office to those who guide the great military conceptions of strategy and tactics. Logistics is dwelt upon first because, while as vital to military success as daily food is to daily work, yet, like food, it is not the work. In this paper attention is to fasten upon the work. Like organization and equipment, logistics underlies achievement; but while nearer the field of battle than those are, and coincident and contemporary with the action of the field, logistics yet is not, so to say, on the fighting-line, nor has it to do with the direction of those movements upon which success and victory immediately hinge.

Evidently the management of such a system of movement and supply requires much experience, and also that training or instruction which in most professions precedes experience and facilitates its acquisition. Similarly, training and experience are requisite in the more advanced stages of the art of war; in strategy and tactics. And it is to be noted closely, as well as clearly, that the object of training and instruction is not merely to mold the individual, but to impress upon each a common type, not of action only, but of the mental and moral processes which determine action; so that within a pretty wide range there will be in a school of officers a certain homogeneousness of intellectual equipment and conviction which will tend to cause likeness of impulse and of conduct under any set of given conditions. The formation of a similar habit of thought, and of assurance as to the right thing to do under particular circumstances, reinforces strongly the power of co operation, which is the essential factor in military operations. Combination and concentration, two leading ideas and objects in war, both indicate unity of energy produced by the harmonious working together—co-operation—of many parts.

Obviously such harmony is not best when merely mechanical, for a mechanical mind is easily deranged in presence of the unexpected. It is the inspiration of common purpose and common understanding which, when the unexpected occurs, supplies the guiding thought to meet the new conditions and bend them to the common end. If this condition be adequately attained, the mind of the commander-in-chief will be omnipresent throughout his command; the most unexpected circumstances will be dealt with by his subordinates in his spirit as surely as though he were present bodily. It is difficult to overestimate the importance of such a result. The captains of individual battle-ships, the commanders of the several corps of an army, have it in them to make or to mar the purposes of the commander-in-chief; not by disaffection, but by lack of comprehension. Lord Howe's entire plan of battle in 1794 was thus wrecked, as was Rodney's on an earlier occasion, by incapacity which previous training should have obviated. In land warfare the twin battles of Gravelotte and St. Privat, in the Franco-German War, gave illustration, one of a subordinate fully comprehending, and consequently not only executing his general's full conception, but developing it even further as opportunity arose; whereas the other, by failure to comprehend, effected merely confusion and disorder, without result.

It is to supply such common understanding and inspiration that war colleges have been instituted. Those who receive the training go forth inbued with a common mode of thought, which latterly has received the name of "Doctrine." There is about this word a suggestion of pedantry which impels to a justification for the use of it. In military operations doctrine, if not given the name, has always existed. When Nelson took his first independent command, three months before the battle of the Nile, he summoned his captains frequently on board his own ship, where he explained to them his proposed methods of action under many possible conditions. This was his doctrine. When the battle came off, each captain understood what he was to do and what the others were to do; and that not mechanically, but with a general idea applicable to all probable circumstances. "I should never have dared to attack as I did without knowing the men, but I was sure each would find a hole to creep in at." Each captain was possessed with the spirit and understanding of Nelson himself.

In like manner before Trafalgar, the *Nelson touch* of which he spoke exultingly was the Nelson doctrine, imparted to the captains severally and collectively, and by them received enthusiastically. "It was my pleasure to find it not only generally approved, but clearly perceived and understood." Collingwood's impatient remark when Nelson made his famous last signal, "I wish Nelson would stop signaling, for we all know what we have to do," is an affirmation of "doctrine" understood. An imperfect comprehension of Rodney's doctrine by the captain whose ship was the pivot of the operation lost the admiral what he considered the greatest opportunity of his life. The absence of "doctrine" is shown by his words subsequently:

I gave public notice that I expected implicit obedience to every signal.made. My eye on them had more dread than the enemy's fire, and they knew it would be fatal. In spite of themselves I taught them to be what they had never been before—officers.

It is to be observed that the eye of the admiral had to be everywhere, just because there was among the officers no spirit of doctrine on which he could rely.

The French word *doctrinaire*, fully adopted into English, gives warning of the danger that attends doctrine; a danger to which all useful conceptions are liable. The danger is that of exaggerating the letter above the spirit, of becoming mechanical instead of discriminating. This danger inheres especially in—indeed, is inseparable from—the attempt to multiply definition and to exaggerate precision; the attempt to make a subordinate a machine working on fixed lines, instead of an intelligent agent, imbued with principles of action, understanding the general character not only of his own movement, but of the whole operation of which he forms part; capable, therefore, of modifying action correctly to suit circumstances. "When I tell Lord Howe to do anything," wrote his senior, "he never asks how it is to be done, but goes and does it." This illustrates the proper relation of a superior to a subordinate. It is not only generous, but sagacious. Hence, in the instruction of war colleges great stress

is laid upon the formulation of orders; in the particular respect that while they are to convey lucidly
to the subordinate the general aim of the operation,
and his own specific share, with such collateral
factors as are necessary for his understanding of the
situation, the guidance is left in his hands. He is
to be told what is to be done, not hampered with
directions how to do it; because the "how" may not
fit a condition he finds before him, but even more
because his own power of independent initiative is
too valuable a military asset to be so repressed.

A curious illustration of the existence of a doctrine,
among seamen not usually suspected of theorizing
but considered specifically practical, is found two
hundred years ago in the express order of the British
Fighting Instructions that an attacking fleet was
first to form on a line parallel with the enemy and
then to steer down upon him, all ships together;
the van to engage the enemy's van, the center the
center, the rear the rear. It was a very bad doctrine;
not least bad in that it took all discretion away from
every one. The one saving clause—unexpressed—
was that a man who fights will always be approved.
Contrast this with Nelson at St. Vincent. It is
true he had received no doctrine from his commander-
in-chief, but he had the equivalent—he perceived
his senior's plan; and, seeing it about to fail, he broke
out of the order and thwarted the enemy's attempt.
Brilliant as this was in an exceptional man, it is
much better that the average man should be equipped

with the understanding which would reach the same result through comprehension. Collingwood, a distinguished example of the average man, was on this occasion close behind Nelson, in the order most favorably situated to imitate him; but he had no doctrine by which to overpass the signals.

It seems self-evident that if a doctrine, as described, is to be valid to the ends of a common spirit and to foster individual power of initiative on certain broad common lines, it must be not only a general principle, or set of such principles, but must be assimilated mentally through numerous illustrations. In other words, it must be based on antecedent experience. Formulated principles, however excellent, are by themselves too abstract to sustain convinced allegiance; the reasons for them, as manifested in concrete cases, are an imperative part of the process through which they really enter the mind and possess the will. On this account the study of military history lies at the foundation of all sound military conclusions and practice. It therefore is the basis, the corner-stone, upon which the instruction of a war college rests. Historical occurrences, analyzed and critically studied, have been the curriculum through which great captains have trained their natural capacity for supreme command. They correspond to the legal cases and precedents which embody and illustrate principles, and so govern legal argument and judicial decision, the struggle and the victory of a court of law.

It is evident on consideration that military precedents derived from history are chiefly valuable as embodying principles, which are to be elicited and then to be applied in circumstances often very different. They are not mere models for a copyist. Two battles will rarely be fought on the same ground; and were the ground the same, the constitution and numbers of the opposing forces will vary. A leading feature in war-college instruction, therefore, necessarily is the constitution of new cases, problems, hypothetical but probable, to the solution of which are to be applied the principles derived from military history. The applicatory system, as it is fitly called, is thus the superstructure, raised upon the basis of experience as embodied in historical military events. It is to be observed that this system, though artificial, reproduces closely the conditions under which military decisions have to be reached in actual war. Each situation that arises in the course of a campaign is a new case, to which the commander-in-chief applies considerations derived from his own experience or from his knowledge of history. It is not meant that these applicatory processes in the field are always conscious efforts of memory, although Napoleon has said that on the field of battle the happiest inspiration is often only a recollection. The exercise of the functions of a trained mind is instinctive, as well in such recollection as Napoleon cited as in decisions which seem wholly personal. Said the great Austrian general, the Archduke Charles:

A general often does not know the circumstances upon which he has to decide until the moment in which it is necessary to proceed at once with the execution of the necessary measures. Then he is forced to judge, to decide, to act with such rapidity that it is indispensable to have the habit of embracing these three operations in a single glance. But that piercing perception which takes in everything at a glance is given only to him who by deep study has sounded the nature of war; who has, so to speak, identified himself with the science.

This is a tribute to the methodical training of faculties. Such training is the peculiar object of the applicatory system—to identify the mind and its habit of action with the art of war, by continuous exercise in dealing with numerous varied instances; a process of repetition which cannot but have the effect that habit always has upon conduct and character. The statement of this effect appeals to the experience of every one. All know how inevitably and unconsciously one repeats the same action under similar circumstances—the "second nature" of the proverb. When this result has been produced in a number of men who act together, there will extend throughout the entire command a unity of purpose and of comprehension which to the utmost possible extent will insure co-operation, because it has already insured a common understanding and habit of action. Thus of the renowned Light Brigade of the Peninsular War, formed under the still more renowned Sir John Moore, it is said that "the secret of its efficiency lay in inculcating correct habits of command in the regimental officers."

The system of discipline, of instruction, and of command formed in the persons of their company officers a body of intelligent and zealous assistants, capable of carrying out the plans and *anticipating* the wishes of their seniors; not merely a body of docile subordinates capable of obeying orders in the letter, but untrained to resolute initiative. The most marked characteristics of Sir John Moore's officers were that when left alone they almost invariably did right. They had no hesitation in assuming responsibility. They could handle their regiments and companies, if necessary, as independent units; and they consistently *applied* the great *principle* of mutual support.

A convenient, because recent, instance of an actual case, which might very well have been constituted as suppositive by an instructor, may be found in the circumstances and conditions of the respective military and naval forces of Japan and Russia before their still recent war. The Japanese authorities had before them the positions of the Russian principal army in Manchuria, the fortified port of Port Arthur, the actual or estimated numbers in the field and in the garrison, the Russian main fleet in Port Arthur, the powerful detachment in Vladivostok, the Russian vessels on the way east at various points; probably also the two or three at Chemulpo, the separation of which at a moment evidently critical indicated an incaution which was doubtless responsible for the exposure also of the main fleet to torpedo attack. Such observed incaution is itself a valuable factor in a military decision. The various facts here given, with the corresponding elements on the Japanese side, stated in a succinct, orderly manner, constitute a problem of exactly the character hypothetically assumed in a war-college problem. When stated, the query follows: Estimate the situation; decide your course of action, which is styled, technically, the Decision; and for its execution formulate your orders to subordinates. The orders to each subordinate will state clearly the situation, the part assigned to himself, with as much information concerning the movements of others engaged in the general operation as will, or may, enable him to act intelligently. What the subordinate is to accomplish—his Mission—is made perfectly clear. How he is to do it is left to his own judgment, partly because the circumstances under which he may have to act can rarely be foreseen, chiefly because reliance can be felt that men brought up with a common vision will do the right thing.

At the war college, the propounding such a problem as the one just cited has been preceded by a course of lectures by men whose previous study and experience have constituted them experts. Each officer under instruction submits two papers: (1) Estimate of the situation, deduced from all the factors, at the close of which is formulated a proposed course of action, which is called the Decision; (2) an order, or set of orders, for putting the decision into execution. The estimate of the situation involves, as a factor, a determination of the proper strategic end to be accomplished; the *ultimate* achievement of which end, whether at once or later, is styled the Mission. Upon this follows consideration of the numbers and disposition of the enemy's forces, and of one's own, as modifying the possibility of immediately accomplishing the mission. Thus Mission defines the end; Decision, the practicable first step. If objection be taken to terms such as mission and decision—or doctrine—the reply is that in all technical treatment technical terms are necessary; and that, when once comprehended, they facilitate discussion, exactly as each foreign word acquired facilitates conversation.

For executing the decision, orders are addressed to each subordinate for his particular part in the combination which the decision requires. Both estimates and orders are then reviewed by the instructor, with criticism and suggestion. Ultimately there is a general discussion among all in full conference. Besides the elucidation which any matter receives from the deliberation in common of several minds, this discussion reacts upon the men engaged. It tends to correct errors, yes; but the great advantage is that principles and illustrations enter into the mind more and more through repetition, not only in the particular discussion of the varied phases of a single case, but by reiteration in many discussions of many cases. For a principle, if correct, cannot but recur repeatedly, steadily deepening its grip. Similarly, reiterated instances of disaster from specific dispositions emphasize warning and give security against errors of like general character.

The value of such a study as that suggested above

for the Japanese is still more recognizable, if we imagine it undertaken by the Russian staff a year before the war began. This will illustrate the vital connection between national policy and military preparation. Upon this the war college strongly insists, and most properly has embodied in its course. International policies is one of the subjects of study. In the United States people are singularly oblivious of the close relation between peace and preparation. Outside of a few officials of the Navy Department, public opinion about naval development does not take into its reckoning any digested consideration of our international exposures. Granting that the Russian officials kept such account as they should of Japanese military and naval preparation, they would have in hand a year before the war the following data: The size, constitution, and disposition of the Japanese army; the numbers and character of the Japanese fleet; the means of transportation available to Japan. As matters of serious dispute existed, these data constituted elements in the problem: how to follow the national policy and yet maintain peace? The Japanese maritime transportation was a large part of the logistics of Japan, as the Siberian Railroad was of that of Russia. The data mentioned, together with the numbers and disposition of the Russian fleets and armies, formed the elements of a problem; to be formulated by a clear and succinct statement of each and all of the factors named. The same demand follows: estimate the situation; formulate your measures to assure peace or to encounter war (which in such a case are identical); issue the orders necessary to execute the measures. If the estimate of the situation had been undertaken by officers with a competent doctrine, the Decision must have been to strengthen the fleet in the Far East; not by vessels proceeding singly—as was done—but by a division as strong as the Baltic ports could send. An estimate of the situation could not but have shown that, although the Russian navy in the aggregate was superior, the division in the Far East was not as strong as, for security, it should be. The whole navy had been divided injudiciously; the first requisite was to reunite it by measures strategically sound, which the despatch of a string of single ships proceeding out was not. The strong naval conviction prevailing in the United States against dividing our battle-fleet between the Atlantic and the Pacific was derived from the war games of the college, testing the strategic situations resulting from such division.

The war game, which has been used for many years at the war college, attacks the same class of problems as does the written "estimate of the situation" and formulation of measures just described. In it the men who write the "estimates," etc., are pitted one against the other as opponents. Similar data are furnished to each: a statement of the conditions as far as known to his superiors—namely, the disposition of the forces on his side, and such account of the enemy's as may be reasonably assumed to be ascertained, but necessarily less full than that of one's own. Each receives also, as from a national government, general instructions, indicating the particular service expected of his command. This is his "mission": *what* he is to do, not *how* to do it. The place of a chess or backgammon board is taken by a large map embracing the scene of operations, upon which are arranged and moved tokens, representing the positions held by both sides, as well as the numbers and successive dispositions of the various forces. The game thence proceeds, move by move. The two contestants occupy separate rooms, while in a third is an umpire who pronounces on each move; whether, by the experiences of war, it is feasible and so permissible.. Within a certain range he decides by his own judgment and accumulated experience, while in other cases there are fixed rules and fixed values assigned to different forces and to different situations. Doubtful cases are under certain conditions submitted to the decision of the dice; thus recognizing Nelson's saying that some allowance must be made for chance, and Napoleon's that war cannot be made without running risks. The game as described embraces all the operations of a campaign, from the start from the base to the collision of the fleets. It thus opens with strategy, which embraces the whole field; narrows gradually till the fleets feel each other's proximity, and are, as it were, manœuvering for advantage on the field, a phase called stratego-tactical; finally, there are the sighting each other and the manœuvers of battle, technically styled tactical. In these last, on the game-board, the rules governing "values" are grounded entirely on the scheme of battle exercises of the battle-fleet in April, 1911; a circumstance illustrating the interconnection between fleet and college, which it may be hoped will be continually greater.

If a nation possesses military positions abroad, many cases in war, and many hypothetical cases at a war college, will present situations which involve both land and sea forces. This added condition constitutes a more intricate problem; but the method of dealing with it, whether by written estimates and subsequent discussion, or by war game, is the same. Owing to more numerous data, the condition is more complex; but the manner of solution will be like.

It will also readily occur that in every war college —and many nations now possess them—the scenes chosen for hypothetical cases to be discussed and solved will be primarily the regions in which general national policies, or particular international relations, make military or naval operations most probable. Historical incidents, *wherever* occurring, are profitable for instruction, for the elucidation or confirmation of the great universal principles of military action; but, for application of those principles, the scenes first to be selected are those where the national forces are most likely to act.

The treatment, purposely discursive because intended to be popular, has made mention of logistics, strategy, tactics, and national policies, giving at greater or less length the character of the subjects thus named, their relation to the purpose of the Naval War College, and the method of treatment; emphasizing the great object of evolving a ·common mode of thought, and a common appreciation of proper military conduct, among all the officers of a navy. There remains one other subject, International Law. In a country full of lawyers and politicians, with a government possessing a President, Secretary of State, and a large corps of ambassadors and foreign ministers, it may be asked doubtfully why naval officers should give time to international law. The reply is that in this extensive system of functionaries the naval admiral or captain is incidentally one; and that, in international law, as in strategy and tactics, he must know the doctrine of his country. In emergencies, not infrequent, he has to act for his superior, without orders, in the spirit and manner his superior would desire. If in war, the war may be complicated by a dangerous foreign dispute arising from action involving neutral rights; or, on the other hand, a neutral unright may be tolerated to the disadvantage of the national cause. In peace, injudicious action may precipitate hostilities; or injudicious inaction may permit infringement of American rights, of persons or of property. The treatment of international law, consequently, is the same as of the more distinctively military subjects—a competent lecturer and lecture system, the posing of problems, their solution by the student, comment and criticism by the teacher, discussion in full conference.

X

WAS PANAMA "A CHAPTER OF NATIONAL DISHONOR"?

In November, 1903, following promptly upon the final rejection of the Hay-Herran Convention by the Senate of the Republic of Colombia, an uprising against the central government of the Republic took place in what was then the Department of Panama. The actual rejection of the treaty was notified to the United States Government by the Colombian Minister to the United States on August 22d, but the Colombian Senate remained in session until October 31st considering the general question of a canal treaty. On that date it adjourned, having taken no step toward a further treaty, but postponing all consideration of the subject to the next meeting of its Congress a year later, October 31, 1904.

On November 3d came the Panama revolt. The day before this occurrence, November 2d, the United States Government, which had abundant warning that an outbreak was imminent upon the rejection of the treaty, had telegraphed its naval officers on both sides of the Isthmus to maintain free and uninterrupted transit; to occupy the line of the railroad, if necessary; and to prevent the landing of any armed force, government or insurgent, at any point within fifty miles of Panama. On November 6th the Republic of Panama, having been declared independent by the insurgents, was recognized as an independent state by the Government of the United States. On November 13th the minister by it appointed was received officially by President Roosevelt; and on December 18th was signed a new Canal Treaty with the new state. This treaty followed the main lines of that which Colombia had rejected; but the Canal Zone was widened from six miles to ten, and the powers of the United States within it were enlarged.

The course of President Roosevelt in these transactions not only was marked by a rapidity and decisiveness which might be characterized as outwardly precipitate, but it secured results extremely advantageous to the United States. Naturally, therefore, the immediate impression produced was equally precipitate, and such as commonly follows where action unusual in kind and seemingly hasty coincides with self-interest. The act was looked upon as dictated only by considerations of profit, and as such was weighed in the balance of untested first impressions as to legality and obligation. The prepossessions thence arising have continued to prevent a clear and unprejudiced weighing of the arguments of legal and illegal; or of those of right and wrong, which do not always coincide with law. Yet an act profitable to one's self may be not only upright, but proper.

In such cases, however, there is an evident necessity that a due respect to the opinions of mankind should lead to a cogent exposition of the reasons for the action taken. Such an exposition was given by President Roosevelt in his annual message to Congress of December 7, 1903, and in a special message of January 4, 1904. A similar exposition was given by Mr. John Hay, then Secretary of State, in his correspondence with General Reyes, the envoy sent by Colombia to remonstrate against the whole course of the United States attendant upon the Panama revolt. It is to be observed that Mr. Hay, while undoubtedly approving of the President's action, was in no official sense responsible for it. All executive responsibility centers in the President, and in him alone. The approval of Mr. Hay, therefore, carries with it the full weight of his known character for probity, moderation, and ability, undiminished by the element of self-defense inseparable from personal accountability.

This is the more important to be observed because the strenuousness of Mr. Roosevelt's character communicates itself to his speech and writings; the vigor of which, when exerted in necessary self-justification, tends rather to confirm the first impression of indefensibleness, produced by the transaction as summarized above. This, undoubtedly, has intensified an opposition which has assumed itself to be distinctively and exclusively moral; which has repudiated as impossible any other standards than its own;

and by confident asseveration has succeeded in determining a very general attitude of the public, as
indicated in the press, at the mouth of which most
men take most of their opinions irreflectively. It
seems, therefore, not unfit to subject the matter anew
to an analysis based mainly upon the official papers,
which probably few have read and fewer studied.
This is the more desirable because Mr. Roosevelt's
action has been condemned recently and unquali-
fiedly by so respectable a citizen as Dr. Leander
Chamberlain,[1] whose article I have occasion to
think was considered unanswerable by an eminent
lawyer.

Dr. Chamberlain's paper may be described as an
impassioned arraignment of the United States, concentrated upon the person of Mr. Roosevelt. It
must be remembered that while the nation and its
President are separate entities, and while the action
of the one may be censurable in the same instance
that that of the other is correct, it nevertheless remains true that the responsibility of the Chief
Executive devolves upon the people, if by them his
act is approved, explicitly or implicitly. Upon this it
follows that examination must extend not only to
the immediate steps and reasons of the national
government in the particular instance, but also to
such other facts as may or should condition the
entire subsequent attitude of the nation. Nothing

[1] *The North American Review*, February, 1912.

has been done by the country to redress or atone for the alleged wrong to Colombia. Therefore—not Mr. Roosevelt alone, but—the nation is at the bar; and the matter for examination is not only the specific step taken and reasons given by the Executive of the day, but also the actual conditions of every kind at the moment of action. These should influence the decision of the nation now as to its responsibility for existing conditions, and as to any reparation assumed to be due.

It is not my intention to take toward Dr. Chamberlain's article the defensive attitude of replying *seriatim* to his successive contentions. I shall adopt the more direct method of stating positively the justifying points of the case for the United States. It is, however, essential to note and to subject to brief comment three propositions which Dr. Chamberlain calls fundamental.

Certain fundamental considerations must be taken into account in any worthy discussion of the conduct of governments. First, that diplomacy now stands committed to "the extending of the empire of law and the strengthening of an appreciation of public justice." Second, that "international jurisprudence is based on the moral law and embodies the consensus of civilized peoples with regard to their reciprocal rights and duties." Third, that "all nations stand on an equality of rights—the old and the new, the large and the small, monarchies and republics." It is, accordingly, in view of these considerations that the Panama imbroglio of 1903 is to be judged.

As regards these positions, any one conversant with the general subject will recognize that they bristle with controversial points and definitions. The third is a commonplace, though necessary to be affirmed. As a sovereign state Colombia is the peer of the strongest and richest. Equally, however, she is liable, like the strongest, to be dealt with according to her deserts. As to the other two—that "diplomacy stands committed, etc.," and that "international jurisprudence is based on the moral law, etc."—the reply is that the basis of international legal decisions is not the ideal that this or that man or men may cherish, but the existing status of law in universal, or at least general, acceptance. The legal basis of judgment is what the law is, not what it ought to be. We long for universal peace, we aim at it and strive for it; but in the present distress we base our preparations upon the serious fact that war, as a means of maintaining international balances, has not been disavowed, and that there is no present prospect of such disavowal. In short, the legality and the morality of the action of the United States are two separate factors, to be separately considered. The legality depends upon the actual state of international law, not on any theory of its derivation or basis. The morality of the transaction is to be treated upon moral grounds. In treatment the two must not be confused by passing loosely from one to the other. If illegal, the fact may impugn the morality of a measure; but the question of legality is separate, and should be kept so.

The present writer has no personal record here to defend, unless it be the imputation likely to be made of a perverted moral twist of intellect and of conscience in believing the course of Mr. Roosevelt vindicable in international law; and still more justifiable in natural equity, as applicable either to the community of states embraced under the domain of that law, or to those nations and populations which still lie without its pale. In general discussion, most dealings with this subject have proceeded on the facile assumption that relations between states not only can hereafter become a matter of purely legal determination—which, being a matter of prophecy or speculation, may be left to one side—but that they actually now are so determinable. This is not the case. In the conflicting relations of independent states a particular action may be lawful—legal—yet not expedient; it may be both lawful and expedient; or it may not square with exact law, yet be essentially just because possessing the highest degree of expediency, that, namely, of doing essential justice between all the parties concerned.

In the case before us the Senate of Colombia had an indisputable legal right to reject the treaty. The question must, therefore, be treated whether the United States had a strict legal right to take the precise steps it did when the Panama revolt affected the *status quo*. It will be similarly necessary to examine and adduce in due course both the legal and moral aspects, recognizing that a transaction may be justifiable from the one or the other stand-point, while not necessarily so from both.

As far as has come under my observation, the entire incident is treated as between Colombia and the United States only. The interest of Panama is never mentioned. This is much as if the intervention of the United States in Cuba, in 1898, should be regarded as a matter between the United States and Spain alone; and from conversation I am inclined to believe that this is the lawyer's point of view, so far as justification of our action is concerned. Yet it is notorious that the suffering of Cuba was a very large factor not only in determining our intervention, but in justifying it. Now, there certainly was not in the Panama district any suffering precisely comparable to that in Cuba; but there was and for three years had continued to be the distraction, misery, and prostration incident to civil war, concerning which the Colombian envoy to Washington, General Reyes, alleged "the weakness and ruin of my country after three years of civil war scarcely at an end."[1] Of this war the Isthmus was a principal scene, the motive being resistance to the central government. The territory of Panama, said General Reyes again, "forms the most important part of the national wealth."[1] Yet, having this importance, it was really an outlying department, separated by long distance from the

[1] *A Digest of International Law*, by John Bassett Moore, vol. iii, pp. 90, 82, Government Printing Office, Washington, 1906.

central government at Bogotá and accessible only by sea, like Cuba. "It is known," wrote Reyes, "that there is no overland way to reach Panama with troops from the interior of Colombia."[1] This, in truth, was the sting of Mr. Roosevelt's order forbidding troops of either party to land within fifty miles of Panama. The measure was decisive. Was it also justifiable? This is, perhaps, the crucial point; for, given the rightfulness of the order, the rest follows up to the recognition of the new state, which must be defended or impeached on other grounds.

In the three preceding years the Isthmus had been constantly the scene of fighting. In 1900 there was continuous fighting about Panama, and British marines had to be landed to protect foreign interests. In 1901 severe fighting took place about Colon; both that city and Panama were seriously threatened by insurgent forces which in November captured Colon. It then became necessary to land American, British, and French naval forces at Colon, which finally was recaptured by the Colombian government.[2] All this imperiled the transit, for which the United States had made itself responsible, and for the security of which it had become necessary at times to acquiesce in the intervention of European force, contrary to the known policy of the nation. These circumstances

[1] Moore's *Digest*, vol. iii, p. 83.
[2] *Encyclopædia Britannica*, Ed. 1910–11, vol. vi, p. 712.

involved the United States directly in the troubles of Colombia; and if a new ownership of Panama would increase its security from disturbance, it would also affect favorably the treaty burden resting upon the United States. Therefore, the contingency of such occasion arising entered fairly into the contingent policy of the United States; the more so that the imminent probability of a revolt became known to it soon after the adverse action of the Colombian Senate upon the treaty was taken.

From this precedent knowledge it has been loosely inferred that the United States was in collusion with the authors of the revolt. It is well, therefore, to quote here Mr. Hay's explicit and categorical denial of such an insinuation made by General Reyes:

Any charge that this government or any responsible member of it held intercourse, whether official or unofficial, with agents of revolution in Colombia is utterly without justification. Equally so is the insinuation that any action of this government prior to the revolution in Panama was the result of complicity with the plans of the revolutionists. The Department sees fit to make these denials, and it makes them finally." [1]

Even without this evidence, the prior knowledge of the United States Government, and the measures taken to be ready at once to meet a probable emergency in which its own interests or those of its citi-

[1] *A Digest of International Law*, by John Bassett Moore, vol. iii, p. 91.

zens might be affected, could not fairly be construed as action accessory to the foreseen revolution. Through officials of its own, that Government had ample information beforehand of the critical condition of affairs at the Isthmus, as well as elsewhere in Colombia. It would have been culpably remiss if it had not taken precautionary steps to be prepared immediately to protect American interests, should such be imperiled, and flagrantly short-sighted, if it had failed to predetermine its own course in the event of such possible contingencies as could be anticipated. Orders consequently were sent to several vessels of war to go to various points where they would be at hand if needed. As far back as 1856 President Pierce took similar contingent action. "I have deemed the danger of the recurrence of scenes of lawless violence in this quarter so imminent as to make it my duty to station a part of our naval force in the harbors of Panama and Aspinwall."[1] It is a frequent anticipative measure. Mr. Hay's denial is conclusive. The United States was not a participant, direct or indirect; but if trouble arose it would be a directly interested party, not merely an intervener from outside. It was interested, not only as formal guarantor of a security which Colombia had repeatedly failed to sustain, but also by an avowed national policy familiarly summarized as the Monroe Doctrine.

Further, this national policy had introduced the

[1] Moore's *Digest*, vol. iii, p. 37.

whole family of European states as parties interested in the canal treaties and in the situation constituted by the rejection of the Convention. Gradually, step by step, the United States had advanced
from a position of joint guarantorship with Great
Britain, of any canal at the Isthmus, to that of
claiming and demanding sole guarantorship for itself;
and from an avowed willingness to see the enterprise aided by foreign capital to an equally avowed
determination that only the United States should
undertake the construction. Such exclusion of
other nations by force—for force it was—necessarily
entails an obligation to them that that which we
forbade their undertaking for the general benefit
should by us be accomplished without avoidable
delay. How admirably this obligation has been
discharged since the authority to do so was obtained from the new Republic of Panama is now a
matter of history; not yet wholly finished, but already with a record which will remain historical.

It is possible that the full development of this
particular element of the situation, which was constituted by our obligation to the other Powers of
the world, may not have passed through the mind
of President Roosevelt, although in his messages
there is clear recognition of an international obligation. But however partially or completely he may
have worked out this specific conclusion, it is valid
for the consideration of the nation in reviewing its
own responsibility *now* for the action of its Chief

Executive *then*. A right action may be doubly right for reasons which may not at the moment have occurred to the agent.

From what has been written, it appears to follow that the transactions, November 2–10, 1903, were no simple matter between Colombia and the United States, but complex. They involved our relations to other nations of the world and to the population of Panama as third parties. Panama was entitled to consideration as really as was Cuba in 1898. She was so entitled, partly because, although the United States was not under treaty obligation to repress domestic disturbance at the Isthmus, Panama was a principal sufferer from the conditions of disquietude which affected the transit; partly because Panama bore to Colombia much the same relation as Cuba to Spain—namely, that of an outlying possession rather than a contiguous and continuous territory. The impossibility of invasion except by sea substantiates this fact; and it is known that Bogotá is the capital because in the districts surrounding the city—in the highlands of the interior—is to be found the bulk of the white population, which at an early date withdrew thither from the hot and unhealthy climate of the coast. In that isolation they have preserved the language, manners, and physical characteristics of their Spanish ancestry, with all its defects and virtues, with less variation than any other Spanish-American state; and thence they governed the remote district of

Panama. It is needless to remark how adverse to the interests of any community is administration by one so distant in time and difficult of access, as well as differing in racial characteristics. Whether or no such considerations were elaborated in the minds of President Roosevelt and his eminent Secretary of State, they remain factors for consideration by the people of the United States in estimating now the essential rectitude of a transaction for which they have become responsible by the approval of tacit sanction.

With this preliminary statement of facts and factors, I address myself now to the question of the technical legal correctness of the action of the United States Government—of President Roosevelt —in forbidding the landing of Colombian armed forces, whether of the government or of the insurrection, within fifty miles of Panama. This was undoubtedly decisive of the issue of the insurrection. It need not have been followed by recognition of the new state. It was open to the United States to say to Panama: "We have insured quiet by excluding national troops. Now we require you to admit them peaceably and to recognize the authority of Colombia." By the exclusion the United States held the whole matter in its hands and stood between the parties as umpire. The intervention— of the fifty-mile order—and the recognition are separate facts; and though in near sequence are not linked.

In a complicated transaction questions of expediency and of legality blend and affect one another practically; but logically they are different, and in discussing either it is necessary to exercise so much mental effort as to exclude for the moment the one not immediately under consideration. As a matter of legal interpretation, under international law, forcible intervention in another country or between two contestant states is a legal right, in the sense that the nation exercising it contravenes no dictum of international law. Abstention from intervention in strictly domestic conflicts is the recognized rule; but it is equally recognized that it is a rule which may have exceptions. The act may be morally right or wrong; it may be expedient or inexpedient; but it is not illegal. By accepted law in this, as in declaring war, the state is its own judge of right. This is the present status of international law. It is evident that, if a state is its own judge as to declaring war, it must be so in any minor exercise of force, although it equally has no legal right to interfere except that of force; the independence of each state forbidding by accepted principle the intrusion of other authority than its own, except that of force. Such a step, however, may become illegal in special cases where the intervening state by treaty has given up its general right in the specific instance. Barring treaty, the United States had a perfect legal right to intervene by force for Panama against Colombia; still more to intervene, in such measure as she deemed necessary, to preserve quiet in a transit in which she was nationally interested. The question remains, Had she by treaty abandoned this right?

The allegation is that she had done so by the treaty of 1846, in the thirty-fifth article of which occur the words now to be quoted, which I believe contain all the stipulation bearing upon this question of legality.

The United States, in order to secure to themselves the tranquil and constant enjoyment of these advantages [before stipulated] and as an especial compensation for the said advantages, and for the favors they have acquired by the fourth, fifth, and sixth articles of this treaty, guarantee, positively and efficaciously, to New Granada, by the present stipulation, the perfect neutrality of the before-mentioned isthmus, *with the view that the free transit from the one to the other sea may not be interrupted or embarrassed*[1] in any future time while this treaty exists; and, in consequence, the United States also guarantee, *in the same manner*, the rights of sovereignty and property which New Granada has and possesses over the said territory.[2]

It will be observed that these words contain two guarantees from the United States to Colombia (at that date called New Granada): (1) the perfect neutrality of the Isthmus; (2) the rights of sovereignty and property which Colombia possessed over it. It must be remembered again that we are dealing now with dry legal construction, not with the morality of any transaction whatever. Legal construction involves the interpretation of phrase-

[1] These words are italicized as showing the particular object, motive, and reason of the treaty.
[2] Moore's *Digest*, vol. iii, p. 6.

ology; and where that is doubtful—where the nego-
tiators have failed clearly to express their meaning—
their purpose, when it is known or can be reasonably inferred, is a determining factor in reaching
decision.   Now, as Mr. Hay argued, the purpose of
the United States in the treaty, in guaranteeing
transit and in guaranteeing possession, had reference solely to the need of the United States to use
the Isthmus for transit in its broadest sense.   The
need had been brought closely home to our national
consciousness in 1846 by the war with Mexico, in
the course of which troops for the Pacific coast had
to be sent by sailing-vessels around Cape Horn.
General Sherman was one who made this trip, and
was by it determined in favor of a canal.

For the above reasons the phraseology of the
treaty where equivocal must be brought to the bar
of this well-ascertained purpose of the United States,
which entered the treaty with the express object of
securing transit for herself and, though incidentally
only, for all other communities.   Doubt as to the
extent of the guarantee of neutrality did arise long
antecedent to 1903.   Colombia, in 1865, had raised
the question whether it extended to domestic insurrection, and whether in such case she could demand
assistance to maintain neutrality.   The United
States decided in the negative.   Mr. Seward, then
Secretary of State, wrote:

The purpose of the stipulation was to guarantee the Isthmus
against seizure or invasion by a foreign power only.   It could not

have been contemplated that we were to become a party to any civil war in that country by defending the Isthmus against another party. As it may be presumed, however, that *our object* in entering into such stipulation *was to secure the freedom of transit across the Isthmus,* if that freedom should be endangered or obstructed, the employment of force on our part to prevent this would be a question of grave *expediency,* to be determined by *circumstances.*[1]

This is a case of interpretation, which not only implies doubt but explicitly rejects a meaning which the words nevertheless might bear. The interest of the United States being one of transit only, not in Colombia as a nation, she was prepared to intervene against domestic seizure only when the security of her transit was endangered, of which she was the judge; the question being one of expediency, not of obligation. This conclusion is based upon the evident purpose of the United States in the negotiations. It is to be noted also that such intervention is not by Mr. Seward's words conditioned by a request from Colombia. The right of originating intervention is preserved by them. So Mr. Gresham, Secretary of State to President Cleveland, telegraphed in 1895, "If for any reason Colombia fails to keep transit open and free, as that Government is bound by treaty of 1846 to do, United States are authorized by same treaty to afford protection." [2]

The question immediately arises whether the

[1] Moore's *Digest,* vol. iii, pp. 37–38. My italics.
[2] *Ibid.,* p. 43.

phraseology of the other guarantee, that of "rights of sovereignty and property," is open to the same construction, as confined to foreign interposition. "Seizure" of territory is a violation of "rights of sovereignty and territory." It will be observed that in the clause of the thirty-fifth article quoted above, the words "in the same manner" occur. The United States guarantees the rights of sovereignty and property in the same manner as it guarantees neutrality of the Isthmus. The words therefore are not to be pressed beyond the interpretation that the object of this guarantee, like that of the other, is security of transit for the United States, which might be endangered or interrupted by conquest or attack of an external enemy, American or European.

Under these conditions the United States in 1903 saw impending again the danger of the renewal of the civil war which, only recently ended, had for three years distracted Colombia and affected transit. This had necessitated frequent interposition of the United States for the security of transit; and had occasioned just that kind of national anxiety and possibility of political entanglements that arise from intestine quarrels in ill-organized countries with which a close political connection exists, whether the connection be of geographical nearness—as recently in Mexico—or of treaty, or of commercial relations. The Eastern question and the Cretan question may be cited appositely as illustrating the same kind of problem in Europe, with consequent international solicitudes; and also as accounting for the fixed policy of the United States that such questions in America shall not be permitted insensibly to draw in European states as active parties to the controversy of the Isthmus, a result to which frequent disturbances tend.

The case of 1903 having arisen, by the well-ascertained fact that preparations for revolt were being made upon the Isthmus if the Hay-Herran Convention were rejected, the question follows, Did the treaty of 1846, because guaranteeing Colombia's rights of sovereignty and property against foreign invasion, also bind legally the United States not to exercise her general international right of armed interference on behalf of her threatened interests ? There was ample precedent for saying that she was not so bound, but was at liberty to act for the security of transit, which was her one specific interest in Colombian territory, to safeguard which the treaty had been made. The occasion not being one of foreign invasion, but of domestic disturbance, the treaty guarantees of enforcing the neutrality of the Isthmus or of resisting a seizure did not apply. This position had been decided nearly forty years before by Mr. Seward. But if the treaty did not apply—in other words, was non-existent as regarded the case in hand —then the general right of international law sanctioning forcible intervention remained; to be determined, as Mr. Seward had said, by considerations of grave expediency governed by circumstances.

In other words, the treaty of 1846 not being applicable, the United States possessed an unimpaired international right to act as her interests demanded. A measure which should wholly bar all access by sea to the Isthmus was entirely within her legal competence. She had a legal right even to take a side if she chose. She did not take a side, because neither Colombian nor Panama forces were to be permitted to land within fifty miles of Panama. Certainly the particular circumstances caused this provision to strike the Colombian forces harder than the insurgents; yet it is quite conceivable that the latter might have received help from beyond sea, for the same has often occurred in similar rebellions. The obligations of neutrality, when they exist, concern only the action taken, not the results of the action. For example, a neutral state forbids its ports to furnish coal to either belligerent. Evidently the effect is worse to the one not possessing coaling-stations near by than to the one which may have such, but this result does not impeach the neutrality of the action.

The order to the United States naval officers not to permit a landing within fifty miles of Panama was, therefore, wholly within the legal competence of the United States. It insured the neutrality of the Isthmus; an expression which means simply that the territory shall not be permitted to be a scene of war. The result was that the insurrection was successful and that the independence of the district of Panama was proclaimed by its people—that is, there was no resistance to the measure by the inhabitants of the district; neither by arms nor by protest. There was no apparent division of sentiment, such as existed in many of the seceding states of our Union in 1861; and it was natural that there should be none, because great interests of the residents were involved in a favorable solution of the canal question, which the action of the Colombian Senate, though perfectly legal, had postponed indefinitely.

The declaration of Panama independence could not but remain effective as long as the United States persisted in its fifty-mile order. Upon this order, in the judgment of the United States, depended the maintenance of tranquillity; so often disturbed of late years that it may fairly be said that a perpetual expectation of disturbance was the normal condition. The question then arises, How far was the United States legally debarred by the treaty guarantee from recognizing a *de facto* situation, dependent upon an attitude she was determined to maintain? The treaty of 1846 stipulated that the United States guarantees the rights of sovereignty and property of Colombia in the Isthmus "in the same manner"— "positively and efficaciously"—as it guaranteed the perfect neutrality of the Isthmus. Here again Mr. Seward, in 1865, writing with no faintest prevision of the conditions of 1903, but envisaging an entirely different problem, expressed the understanding of the United States as to the obligations of the treaty. Mr. Seward's words were based upon the opinion of the then Attorney-General, which Seward adopted.

Neither the text nor the spirit of the stipulation in that article, by which the United States engages to preserve the neutrality of the Isthmus of Panama, imposes an obligation on this government to comply with a requisition [like that referred to above]. The purpose of the stipulation was to guarantee the Isthmus against *seizure or invasion by a foreign power only*.[1]

Mr. Hamilton Fish, Secretary of State, in 1871 expressed a similar opinion:

A principal object of New Granada in entering into the treaty is understood to have been to maintain her sovereignty over the Isthmus against any attack *from abroad*. That object has been fully accomplished. No such attack has taken place, though this Department has reason to believe that one has upon several occasions been threatened, but has been averted by warning from this Government as to its obligation under the treaty.[2]

In the face of these utterances, it seems evident that there is no ground whatever for the assertion upon which Dr. Chamberlain rests his impeachment of the action of 1903. Dr. Chamberlain writes:

Since the paramount issue in the case of both the neutrality and sovereignty which the United States guaranteed was the safeguarding of the transit, there was a valid implication that the United States, on due occasion and especially at New Granada's request, would give aid against transit interference from any source whatever, whether foreign or domestic.[3]

---

[1] Moore's *Digest*, vol. iii, p. 48. My italics.
[2] *Ibid.*, p. 27. My italics.
[3] *The North American Review*, February, 1912, p. 150.

So far from a valid implication, there was, on the part of the United States, an explicit repudiation of such obligation; and as Colombia during the years since 1865 had acquiesced in this interpretation, by not denouncing the treaty, the understanding between the two Governments was complete in this particular.

The seizure of the Isthmus in 1903 was not the act of a foreign Power, but of Colombian citizens; and the proclamation of independence was by the same body that effected the seizure. The seizure clearly was not of the character against which the United States by long precedent pronouncement had confined its guarantee; for it was not by foreign act, but by domestic. The sovereignty of Colombia had disappeared *de facto* before a domestic insurrection. The legal question then remaining was whether such act should be recognized by foreign states, and when. Recognition by a foreign state undoubtedly gives moral help to an insurgent, and it therefore should not be given lightly; but it is not legally operative between the parties at strife. In fact, recognition, as distinct from active aid, is not operative at all in establishing the independence of a new state, either legally or effectually. The United States dates its independence, not from the recognition by France and Spain in 1778, but from its own declaration, in 1776, as the legal origin. Great Britain did not acknowledge this independence nor cease from her efforts to subdue the United

241

States because of the recognition by France and Spain; and these countries did not effect independence by recognition, though they subsequently did so by armed intervention in the quarrel.

By international law recognition by a foreign state is legally discretional with that state—a matter of national policy and of national determination as to time and circumstances. Ordinarily the decision rests upon the establishment of a *de facto* government, ascertained to be so by organization and continuance; but there is no constraint in law that these two indications must be exacted, or that a *de jure* fact of the wishes and rights of the people may not determine the action of foreign states. The status of Crete since 1897—not political independence, but political autonomy under the nominal suzerainty of Turkey—is due to the action of the great Powers expelling the Turks; after a series of revolts, as in Panama, had demonstrated that quiet could not otherwise be had.

I have tried so far to confine my consideration to the strict letter of the law; to obligation, positive and negative, as involved in the treaty of 1846. Neither by temperament nor by conviction am I inclined ordinarily to exact the strict letter of the bond. I could not have sided decisively with either Shylock or Portia in their literal interpretations. But as the subject under discussion presents itself to me, the question is whether the United States, by the specific undertakings of the treaty of 1846,

had divested itself of its general rights under international law. The frequent assertion that the relations of states are as susceptible of legal definition
and enforcement as those of individual men appears
to me extravagant, as to both fact and reason; but
I do hold that a treaty is a promise, and that its
ascertained stipulations are obligations not only
legal, but moral, having the force of promise. In
such case the determination of action depends upon
ascertainment of the thing promised. No question
of expediency, however plausible, not even of the
welfare of a third party, is to me admissible, unless
under circumstances so exceptional that none such
occurs to me now. I certainly do not hold that any
advantage to the United States or to Panama could
be advanced to justify the action of 1903, if certainly
in contravention of the treaty.

If not in contravention, then the United States
had liberty to take any action she saw fit under her
general international legal rights as a State. The
question then was not one of law, but of morals; and,
except in case of absolute right and wrong, morals
in the case of nations—less frequently in that of
individuals—is often a matter of expediency. "The
greatest good of the greatest number" is a moral
aim, to be guided by considerations of morality and
of expediency. The right to property is not an absolute right; it is not unconditioned, but conditioned.
Municipal law, therefore, permits deprivation of
property for the good of the community. The meas-

ures of the United States caused Colombia to lose property. If the action which so resulted was legal, its rectitude otherwise is to be judged by moral considerations; and these are to be applied not to the facts of the moment only, but also to those anterior, if furnishing a continuous, consistent record. The good of the United States; the national self-interest, which singularly enough is considered by many the sole justifying reason for national interventions; the good of Panama; the good of foreign states, American or non-American; the good—or evil—to Colombia herself; the obligations following upon a systematic policy pursued by the United States in years past, which not only reserved the canal control to herself alone, but insistently excluded all other Powers capable of such control; all these factors enter as considerations in deciding whether the course of the United States was proper. It is always to be remembered, as before said, that the question now is no mere criticism of a past action of a single man, but a determination whether the United States people have been and still are the perpetrators of an unatoned wrong.

Positions like the Isthmus of Panama cannot be considered on a footing merely of uni-state property. They belong essentially to the world, because the world has need of them. The accident of possession undoubtedly gives particular claims to consideration and remuneration; and both consideration and remuneration were tendered and accepted by the Hay-

Herran Convention. To this the Colombian Senate opposed the Colombian Constitution as forbidding cession of sovereignty over national territory. Mr. Hay replied that the Convention actually secured such sovereignty, conceding to the United States only a limited control for police and sanitation, indispensable to the construction and management. The clause in the Convention to this effect quoted by Mr. Hay runs:

> The United States freely acknowledges and recognizes this sovereignty [of Colombia] and disavows any intention to impair it in any way whatever, or to increase its territory at the expense of Colombia.

In short, the United States required, not political sovereignty, but the administrative control of the ground to be occupied by a great industrial enterprise undertaken by it, just as any business corporation requires control of its own grounds. This does not impair the rights of sovereignty, any more than a lease impairs the property rights of an owner.

In any case the constitution of a country is valid to itself alone; it is not a reply in international contentions. When Italians were executed by popular uprising in New Orleans, it was no reply to Italy that the Constitution of the United States left the central Government no power to punish a crime committed in Louisiana. A street for the world needed to be opened through Colombian property; and Colombia could not present her constitution as a valid bar. Had immediate steps been taken to remedy the difficulty, something might be said for delay; but the Colombian Congress, without providing any bases for the reopening of negotiations, adjourned for a year, during which time the matter was "hung up." Not even a beginning at amendment would be made. Under such circumstances the "to-morrow" of Spanish tradition became portentous, and is a fair matter for present consideration as to the present accountability of the American people.

I refrain from considering the grosser pecuniary motives alleged to have influenced the Colombian Senate. That such were existent and operative will, I think, be the conclusion of those who will read attentively the messages of President Roosevelt and the correspondence of Mr. Hay and General Reyes. Though not necessarily determinative of moral judgment, because possibly not morally wrong in men making a bargain for their country, even if evidently narrow and shortsighted, the facts have a sinister appearance and bear upon the general verdict touching the moral propriety of the United States' action. But there is another allegation; not against the Colombian Senate, but against the Executive which arranged the Hay-Herran Convention and submitted it as signed for the approval of the Senate. This I quote textually from Mr. Hay. After stating at length certain actions of the Colombian Government, which he claimed were in direct contravention of agreements in the treaty, which agreements had been accepted after full discussion of the points involved, Mr. Hay wrote:

This state of affairs continued until General Fernandez, in charge of the Ministry of Finance [that is, Secretary of the Treasury to the Colombian Government], issued, more than a month before the Congress was convoked [in special session] and more than two months before it met, a circular to the Bogotá press, which, as Mr. Beaupré[1] reported, "had suddenly sprung into existence," inviting discussion of the convention. The circular in substance stated, according to Mr. Beaupré's report, that the [Colombian] Government "had no preconceived wishes for or against the measure"; that it was "for Congress to decide," and that Congress would be largely guided by "public opinion." In view of what the government had already done, it is not strange that this invitation to discussion was followed by violent attacks upon the convention, accompanied by the most extravagant speculations as to the gains which Colombia might possibly derive from its rejection.[2]

In brief, the Colombian Executive, having after prolonged discussion entered into an agreement with the United States, sought itself to overturn this in popular opinion, as conducive to rejection by the Senate. In this it succeeded. A public act of a Secretary of the Treasury is the act of the Government of which he is part, unless by it repudiated. Although this measure in itself would not affect the moral obligation of the United States to act with due consideration of all interests concerned, it did effectively dispose of any claim of Colombia to special consideration as especially affected. Mr.

[1] The American Minister to Colombia.
[2] Moore's *Digest*, vol. iii, p. 98.

Hay's comment on this transaction will commend itself, I think, to most men:

> Treaties are not definitely binding till they are ratified; but it is a familiar rule that, unless it is otherwise provided, they are binding on the contracting parties [in this case the two governments] from the date of their signature, and that in such case the exchange of ratifications confirms the treaty from that date. This rule necessarily implies that the two governments, in agreeing to the treaty through their duly authorized representatives, bind themselves, pending its ratification, not only not to oppose its consummation, but also to do nothing in contravention of its terms.[1]

What would the British or French governments or our own people have thought if, after the Arbitration Treaties of 1911 were signed, the United States Government had proclaimed to its public, through the general press, that it invited discussion of the points to which the Senate afterward refused consent, and was indifferent whether they were accepted or not.

In conclusion, it is beneficial to observe that the summary ejectment of Colombia from property which she could not improve herself, and against the improvement of which by another she raised frivolous obstacles, is precisely in line with transactions going on all over the world; to the great distress of many worthy people who think that law should, or can, settle all matters, binding nations in links of iron. India, Egypt, Persia, Tripoli, Tunis, Algiers,

[1] Moore's *Digest*, vol. iii, p. 96.

Morocco, all stand on the same general basis as Panama. The world has needed them; and technical possession by legal prescription has fallen, still falls, and should continue to fall, before the advance of the world when the owners are unable or unwilling to improve, or to confer security.

Law is a valuable instrument; invaluable is a more fitting word. But it is only an instrument, it is not a principal. It is a contrivance, a means, not an end. Man is not for law, but law for man. That France in eighty years' occupancy has raised the commerce of Algiers from one million dollars to two hundred millions; that in Tunis in thirty years the increase is from eight millions to forty millions, and that in the same time two thousand miles of good road have been built; the benefits done by Great Britain to Egypt; all these do not so much justify the new administrators in their original action as condemn the old as worthless cumberers of the ground, and therefore rightfully dispossessed. The horrified plea of legal possession violated is in such cases a mere figment of law. It illustrates what has been already said: that Law is a means, not an end; a good servant, but a bad master. So in Panama. Not even the consummate results of the American occupation, in sanitation, in maintaining order, in advancing the canal, with its promise to the world's future, are so complete a justification for the action taken as is the miserable and barren record of the former owner, the Republic of Colombia.

It is sometimes urged: Would the United States
have acted thus in the case of a strong state? The
question posed by the word "strong" is one not of
right, to which this discussion is limited, but of
expediency. In 1911 France, Germany, and Great
Britain, all strong states, maintained severally what
each considered right; but their course was modified
by expediency, formulated by diplomacy, and based
upon armament. The reply to the query, however,
is that necessity for such action rarely arises with
strong states, if the word "strong" be correctly defined. A strong state is one that maintains habitu-
ally peace and security within its borders and im-
proves its possessions. Turkey, exclusive of nominal
dependencies, has 27,000,000 people. Is Turkey a
strong state? Holland has under 6,000,000, Belgium
little over 7,000,000. Who ever thinks of controlling
their domestic concerns? Yet even Belgium has had
occasion to notice that if sovereignty be abused in a
matter of world concern—as in the Congo Free
State—the world will call her to account, just as
Peru is now being summoned to account for the
rubber atrocities, though Peru is a weak state. The
Isthmus of Panama, because of its interoceanic pos-
sibilities, was and is a world concern in so far that if
maladministrated the world will interfere. If the
United States do not give good administration and
security she will hear from the world, though she is
a strong state.

INDEX

ALGIERS, 11, 102, 114, 140, 248.

Arbitration, International: possesses principle of development, 1; tendency to become compulsive and to undermine nationality, 1, 7; originally an instrument of diplomacy, to be used at will, 2; analogy of, to Socialism, 5, 10; query as to powers of a tribunal of, 6; defect in present powers of tribunal, yet danger in increase of powers, 7; preponderant aim of, is merely to escape the material losses of war, 8; contrast between, and natural forces, illustrated, 8, 13; force and, opposite in idea, but not mutually destructive, 10; armaments and, contrasted methods, 11, 13; law, ultimate expression of, 12; antecedent rejection of, by Australia, 25, 170; unlimited, between United States and Great Britain, mentioned, 15, 29, 30–32, 87, 88, 90; distinction between diplomacy and, 36; inadequacy of judicial, in questions of national policy, illustrated, 39–45; dangers of usurpation by a Court of, 48–53; inferior efficacy of, as compared to force, in certain cases, 50–54, 64–66, and in history of United States, 54–56; not adequate to all diplomatic settlements, 78, as illustrated by Monroe Doc-

trine, 79–80, and by Panama Canal Zone, 93–95; essentially opposite to diplomacy in idea and methods, 83; "vital interests" and "national honor" reserved from, 88–90; essential element in treaties of general judicial, 91–93; utterance of German Chancellor concerning general, 95; other instrument than judicial required, 97–99; outworn laws a danger in, 99; as also inadequately developed law, 100, 111, 112, 114, 123; illustrated by conditions preceding Monroe Doctrine, and by development of the Doctrine, 100–105; function of, is legal decision, 112; as to exclusion of Asiatics, refused by Australia, 170–171; armaments and, chapter i.

Armament, and Armaments: the ultimate expression of natural forces, 8; and the embodiment of national power of self-assertion, 9, 137, 139; effect of suppression of, 10; notably in War of Secession, 127; represents aggregation of the national powers of every kind, 11, 124; effect in maintaining peace, 13, 127; dependence of European civilization upon, 14; increase of German, 15–18, 22 (and note), 58, 62, 173; increase of British, 20, 21; illustrations of effect of British naval, 23, 26, 27; purpose of German naval, 29, 32, 57, 62, 63, 69; increase of Austrian naval, 22, 28, 82; onerousness of, but contemporary ability to bear, 33–35; economic view of, 37; question for United States, as regards naval, 67, 70–72, 76, 77; an incident of diplomacy, 81; of European countries, less for self-protection than to insure exterior rights, 113, 116, 123; thesis of *The Great Illusion* concerning, 122, 124, 131; attitude of Canada toward, 159, 172; and of Australia and New Zealand, 169, 173, 175; utilization of, the most vital of military questions, 196; and the special study of War Colleges, 196–215.

Australia, 73, 79, 80, 153, 158, 159, 161, 167–175, 179, 180.

Austria-Hungary, annexation of Bosnia and Herzegovina by, 6, 64–66, 85, 111, 175; naval development in, 22, 28, 82; territorial advance of, east of Adriatic, 24.

BALANCE OF POWER IN EUROPE, 23, 24, 25, 86, 115, 145.

Boer Republics, attempted recognition of, at first Hague Conference, 52–54.

Bosnia and Herzegovina, 6, 64, 66, 85, 111, 175.

Bulgaria, 6, 66, 85.

CANADA, 31, 73, 153, 159–161, 168; strong opposition to development of navy in French provinces of, 159; naval effect upon, of Panama Canal, 160; inferior attachment of, to imperial connection, as compared with Australia, 160, 172; feeling in, as to Asiatic

immigration, 171; commercial relation of, to Panama Canal, 178.

Chamberlain, Dr. Leander, condemning action of United States in Panama (1903), 221, 222, 240.

Chancellor of the German Empire (von Bethmann Hollweg), 29; quoted, 95, 138.

Christian, Church and Civilization, characteristics of, 115–120, 150; separate spheres of Church and State, 118, 119.

Churchill, Winston, British First Lord of the Admiralty, quoted, 139.

Civilization, principle of nationality has played great part in history of European, 1; constitutional basis of European, is the sovereignty of the state, 2, 4, 5; contrasted powers of European and non-European, 8–10; rivalry internal to European, gage of, 11; dependence of European, upon the energy of which armaments are an essential element, 14; consequences of slackening of such energy, 14, 35; tendency shown toward such slackening, 106; states of European, are a community of business organizations, 107; American, derived from European, 107, 179; outward impulse of European, results from internal competitions, 115–119; disarmament of European, means its downfall, 120; between states of European, questions of Tripoli, Morocco, etc., are not legal in character, 123; results of European, in Algiers and Tunis, 140; European, will be weakened by decay of sentiment of nationality, 143; efficiency for corporate action confined most-

INDEX

ly to European, 161; effect of Panama Canal upon spread of European, in Pacific, 159–164, 167–172, 175, 179.

College, the Naval War, Chapter ix.

Colombia, Senate of, rejects Hay-Herran convention, 218, 224; relation of, to Panama, 218, 225–230; characteristics of inhabitants of, 230; treaty of 1846 between United States and, 232–237, 239, 240–242; legal right of United States to intervene in 1903, 232; action of Executive of, while Hay-Herran convention pending, 246–248.

Conference, the First Hague, 50–54.

Crete, and Cretans, 6, 7, 64, 65, 66, 236, 242.

Cuba, 45–48, 55, 86, 97, 111, 155, 164, 225, 226, 229, 230.

"DECISION," technical military term, defined, 210, 211.

Defense, British Committee on Imperial, 73–77; Council of National, proposed for United States, 76, 77.

Diplomacy, Arbitration an instrument of, 2; force at basis of combinations of, 29, 32, 36, 63, 65, 66, 81, 84; international adjustments the work of, 36; obstacles to substitution of judicial arbitration for, 42; illustrated, 42–54; arranges and adjusts, where a tribunal can only pronounce, 66; in this more efficacious than law, as an instrument of policy, 66, 84–86, 91, 92, 96, 97, 99, 101, 103, 104, 111, 112; possesses an elasticity which Law lacks, 78; Armament an instrument of, 81; is the real object of attack by advocates of un-

limited arbitration, 83; General Schofield's mission of, 105; law-making a function of, 112; increasing part played by, in commercial activities of nations, 176; and Arbitration, Chapter ii.

"Doctrine," technical military term, defined and illustrated, 202–206, 211.

FISH, HAMILTON, Secretary of State, quoted as to Treaty of 1846 with Colombia, 240.

Force, and Forces, influence of, in promoting arbitration, 8; of European civilization, as a whole, dependent upon competition between forces of the several states, 9–10, 114–116, 120, 123, 142, 143; arbitration and, opposite in idea, but not mutually destructive, 10; results from natural, more permanent than from artificial regulation, 13; possession of military, does not necessarily imply war, 16, 63–66; German dependence on military, 29, 32; possession of, a national responsibility, 30; War is ultimate expression of, 37; underlies Diplomacy, 36, 63–68, 72–77, 81, 84, 101; underlies Law, and progress, 39, 51, 54, 56, 97–99, 106, 118, 138–142; a legitimate factor in international settlements, 84–90; lies behind Monroe Doctrine, 86, 105; an inevitable factor in international balances, 106; of concentrated capital as real as that of armies, 107; part of, in civil affairs, 107; "Protection" is simply the use of, 108, 113; achievements of, by war, 109–110; or otherwise, 111, 112, 114; in international matters takes line of least

253

INDEX

tary of State, quoted, 46, 220, 227, 233, 245, 246, 247.

Illusion, The Great, 110, 114; Chapter vi.

Immigration, Asiatic, inevitable result of, if allowed in America, 8; settlement of question of Japanese labor, 91, 163; Australia's attitude toward, 170.

Italy, in Tripoli, 12, 85, 123, 138, 139–141, 146; consummation of unity of, 24, 51, 135, 142; the Papacy and, 50–52; subjects of, executed in New Orleans, 245.

JAPAN, adoption of European civilization by, 9, 117, 161; indemnity demanded from Russia by, 21; benefit to, from British alliance, 26; present position of, in Manchuria, 32; immigration from, to United States, 91, 163 (and note); motives of, in war with Russia (1904), 110, 111, 112; in Hawaiian Islands, 164; war with Russia, 165, 166, 186, 189, 194, 209, 210.

LAW, principles of, sought to be imposed upon arbitration, 3, 8, 31, 83; arbitration implies, 11, 12; frequent inapplicability of, to disputes, 12, 13, 31, 32, 33, 39–42, 45–48, 50–55, 65, 66, 78, 79–83, 86, 97–99, 100–103, 123; essential opposition of method between Diplomacy and, 36, 83, 84, 92, 98, 99, 103, 104, 111; force underlies, 39, 106, 107; Monroe Doctrine does not rest upon, 39–42, 79–83, 87, 88, 100–103; Doctrine is a policy, not a, 105; qualifications imposed upon, by national policy, 81, 88–90, 139, 194; in inter-

national effect, may be exasperating rather than conciliatory, 96, and in national, 97–99; lacks elasticity necessary to adjustments, 99; inadequacies of, 112, 114–116, 146; an incubus, except as, 117; may become a fetich, 117; international, reasons for place of, in courses of the Naval War College, 216; is a valuable instrument, but not a principal; a means, not an end, 249; deficiencies of, as an instrument in International Adjustments, Chapter iv.

Lloyd-George, Mr., quoted, on "vital interests," "national honor," and "prestige," 89.

Logistics, military term, defined and illustrated, 197–201; derivation of, 197; Japanese and Russian, in war of 1904–05, 212.

"MISSION," technical military term, defined, 210, 211.

Monroe Doctrine, mentioned, 24, 175, 195, 228; a matter of policy, not of law, 32, 39–42, 82, 87, 100–105; attitude of Great Britain toward, 43, 92, 93; of Germany, 40–43; specific danger to, if Germany should acquire naval base in 'Caribbean, 44; claim founded only on national security, 67; is a formulated principle, 68, 102; successive developments of, are applications of a principle, 68, 101–103, 228, 236, 244; illustrates deficiencies of Law, 79–81; analogous doctrines elsewhere, 79–82; is an instance of local power resisting intrusion of distant power, 86; characterized as a "domestic" policy, 87; applies to islands geographically American,

255

92 (note); General Schofield's foreign mission, 105; an object of, to localize non-American disputes by excluding from America, 132, 138; succinct purpose of, 138.

Morocco, 4, 10, 11, 79, 102, 111, 114, 123, 127, 137–139, 141, 248.

NATIONALITY, and Nationalities: principle of, has played great and beneficent part in history of European civilization, 1, 48, 141–144; sentiment of, is a conservative force, 2; sentiment of, exemplified in course of United States Senate upon treaties of arbitration, 3, 4; Socialism logically opposed to, 5; armaments the embodiment of the spirit of, 9, 127; compulsory arbitration will destroy spirit of, 10; strong prepossessions of, in international disputes, 31, 95–96, 124–126; tendency of arbitration to trench upon, 48–50; illustrated at First Hague Conference, 50–54; competition between, makes for soundness of the international community, 84–86, 145; assertion of British, by Mr. Lloyd-George, 89, and by Mr. Winston Churchill, 139; exemplified in "Protection," 108, 113; effect upon sentiment of, produced by external effort, 128–130; results from establishment of German, 133–135, 146–149, and of Italian, 135; Turkey not a, 135; in the Morocco question, 138; assertion of German, by Chancellor of the Empire, 138; weakening of, in Europe, will weaken European civilization for collision with Asiatic, which impends, 143;

present strength of sentiment of, 144, 163 (and note); sentiment of, in war, 153; effect of sentiment of, in future of Pacific, 161–164, 167–172; asserts itself in commercial development, 176.

Navies as International Factors, Chapter iii.

Navy, and Navies: increase of German, 17–20, 22 (and note), 57–59, 173; effect of German increase of, upon Great Britain, 20, 21, 23, 26, 27, 28; a good foundation of financial credit, 21; increase of Austro-Hungarian, 22–23, 28; effect of superiority of British, a century ago, and consequent maxim thence deduced, 23–25; effect of British, in Russo-Japanese and Boer wars, 26; dependence of Australia upon, 26; determinate principle underlying increase of German, 57, 61–63, 69; principle underlying British increase of, is vague, 61–62; no recognized principle governing increase of, in United States, 59, 63; national and international functions of, 66; numbers and constitution of, should be determined by international considerations, 67; supreme international question concerning, for United States, 67; could become a settled policy like Monroe Doctrine, 68, 69; instructed public opinion necessary for continuous policy as to, 69; strength of, not a purely naval question, but chiefly one of foreign policies, 69; appropriate function of Naval Committees as to, 70; function of Foreign Affairs Committees, and of Executive, as to, 71–74; proper organization of a Commission, or Council, of National Defense, 74–77; effect of British, upon national economical progress, 122, 132; effect of war with Spain, and of Panama Canal upon United States', 155; reciprocal relations of fortifications and, 156–157, 173, 174, 182, 183, 187–90, 192, 194; Canadian hesitancies as to building, 159, 160, 172; effect of Panama Canal upon United States', 157, 164–167, 177, 182, 184–186, 192–195, and upon British, 160; Australian measures as to, 172; Lord Kitchener on primary relation of British, to security of the Empire, 173; should not be the sport of local politics, 177; of United States, should be second in force only to that of Great Britain, 180, 195; determinative effect of, in development of Pacific, 180; impolicy of dividing United States', between the two oceans, 185–186, 213; permanent inferiority of, means ultimate defeat, 194; mobility, distinguishing characteristic of, 198.

New Zealand, 73, 79, 80, 153, 159, 167–175, 179, 180.

Open Door, the, analysis and definition of, 115; mentioned, 123, 138.

Panama, and Panama Canal Zone, 4, 12, 13, 32, 50, 56, 67, 93, 94, 95, 130, 155; peculiar interest of United States in, 157; contrasted with interest of Great Britain in Suez, 158; essentially part of United States coast-line, 158; twofold effect of, upon sea-power in

Pacific, 159, and following; like Suez, gateway to Pacific, 177; is now United States territory, 181; not to be regarded as an isolated position, but in relation to other conditions, 182, 192–193; revolt of, against Colombia, 218, 224; Republic of, recognized by United States, and Treaty with, 219; effect upon, by continual civil commotion, 225–227; interest of European states in, 228, 244, 250; right of United States to intervene in, 229–237; Isthmus of, cannot be regarded merely as property of a single state, 244, 248, 250.

Panama Canal and Sea Power in Pacific, Chapter vii.

Panama, "A Chapter of National Dishonor?", Chapter x.

Papacy, the, at the First Hague Conference, 50–52.

Philippines, 13, 49, 109, 111, 166, 168, 177, 182, 187.

Pierce, Franklin, President United States, quoted as to precaution of force at Isthmus of Panama, 228.

Policy, national, naval, and military: German, 15, 16, 19, 22 (and note), 32, 57–59, 65, 96, 173; British, 20, 23, 27, 62, 89, 92–93, 101; British, accepts Monroe position, 43, 92; effect of Arbitration Treaties upon, 29; Monroe Doctrine a national, 32, 41, 42, 68, 81, 82, 87, 101–104, 105, 132, 181, 195; as affected by party government, and where Executive preponderates, 60–63; annexation of Bosnia and Herzegovina by Austria, 64–66, 84; United States naval, dependent upon what can be willingly conceded

THE END